CONSTRUCTIONS

CONSTRUCTIONS

Michael Frayn

WILDWOOD HOUSE LONDON

FIRST PUBLISHED 1974

© 1974 BY MICHAEL FRAYN

WILDWOOD HOUSE LTD, 1 WARDOUR STREET, LONDON W1V 3HE

ISBN 0 7045 0107 4

FILMSET BY BAS PRINTERS LIMITED, WALLOP, HAMPSHIRE
PRINTED BY BIDDLES OF GUILDFORD
BOUND BY WM BRENDON, TIPTREE, ESSEX

CONSTRUCTIONS

[1] The complexity of the universe is beyond expression in any possible notation.

Lift up your eyes. Not even what you see before you can ever be fully expressed.

Close your eyes. Not even what you see now.

[2] Our notations are by their very nature simpler than what they denote. This is the point of them: to reduce the multiformity of the world to common forms, so that things can be brought into a logical and conceptual relationship with each other.

[3] For as much of the time as possible, we shut ourselves up in our notations and refuse to come out. It's when we are forced to observe and think afresh that the discrepancy between this simplicity and that complexity overwhelms us.

[4] By our inmost animal nature we are readers. We read the world around us continuously, obsessively, necessarily. Reading our notations is a late specialization of a general skill.

[5] Our reading of the world and our mastery of notations are intimately linked. We read the world in the way that we read a notation – we make sense of it, we place constructions upon it. We see in the way that we speak, by means of selection and simplification. I should like to end up by saying (gnomically, metaphorically) that

we read the world by developing from it a kind of notation of itself. You see your hand by seeing it *as* a hand. You see the branches of the tree against the blueness of the sky by seeing *that* the branches of the tree are against the blueness of the sky. I say to you (in all the relative simplicity of the language notation), 'The leaves on the tree are shaking in the wind,' and, given a context, you take the sense of this (directly – you don't have to form a mental picture to understand what I say). There is an unremarked parallel between what you do here and what you do when you look at the tree yourself, in all the immeasurable complexity of the natural world, and (without formulating any thought in words) take the sense that its leaves are shaking in the wind.

[6]   We are significance-seeking organisms.
      We seek out significance from our environment as we seek out food. We crave meaning as we crave warmth.
      If we didn't find significance and meaning we should find food or warmth, either.

[7]   We look at the taciturn, inscrutable universe, and cry, 'Speak to me!'

[8]   We can't *stop* reading. Compulsively we find ourselves reading significance into dreams (we construct a science upon it); into tea-leaves and the fall of cards. We look up at the shifting vapours in the sky, and see

faces, lost cities, defeated armies. Isolated in the dark, with nothing to hear and no surfaces to touch, we hallucinate reading-matter.

Our craving becomes generalized – for 'the meaning of life'. The only answers we can suggest are either banal or foolish; but the expectation of finding them retains its dogged charm.

[9] Our ability to read the phenomena around us depends upon our ability to differentiate them. So, obsessively, we classify and order. And we judge, and rank by merit. We find everything better or worse, more beautiful or less beautiful, socially superior or inferior, approvable or disapprovable. We discover for ourselves universal orienting principles, like the earth's magnetic field, by which we can set course through whatever turns up on our travels – desert, mountains or ocean; sunlit day or starless night. Surrounded by the grey ocean, we have to be able to say that this part of it is to the north of us, while *this* part, though it looks indistinguishable, is to the south.

[10] If we lived alone in a featureless desert we should learn to place the individual grains of sand in a moral or aesthetic hierarchy. We should long to find the greatest grain of sand in the world, and even (in order to find a fixed point of orientation in time as well as in space) the all-time greatest grain of sand; the grain of sand whose discovery changed our whole understanding of grains of sand for ever.

[11] It is this need to impose order that is the attraction of
      the pathetic fallacy; pathos is significance. We have a
      whole range of conventions, in literature and in
      everyday conversation, which permit us to extract
      emotional flavouring from the most irrelevant of
      contingencies. The occurrence of events at different
      times, but in the same place: 'The street where the
      man was shot – I passed it not two weeks previously!
      And the place the shot was fired from was *almost
      exactly* where forty years ago the man's grandfather
      used to run a jellied eel stall!' And the simultaneity of
      events in different places: 'As she took the milk and
      biscuits across the hall into the nursery, she glanced at
      the clock on the press. It was exactly 3.10. At the same
      moment in Dallas one of the secret service men in the
      motorcade glanced at his watch. They were just
      approaching the underpass in front of the Texas Book
      Depository . . .'
         They do seem to bear some charge of meaning, these
      incomplete space-time correlates. Odd, when you come
      to think about it, that we don't allow pathos to events
      which occur at the same latitude, with only twenty or
      thirty degrees of longitude keeping them apart.

[12] Our desire to blame and to be blamed is often an
      attempt to impose meaning upon events which offer
      none, or only an obscure and confusing one. For some
      impossibly complex and circumstantial conjunction of
      reasons, a lorry plunges into a crowd; an economic

policy fails; a battle is lost. Our instinct is at once to find someone whose behaviour can now be reinterpreted as negligent or criminal, so that the event can be read into the world's great underlying pattern of cause and effect. A falling tree kills one's child. A meaningless event, but of such terrible consequence that one can't bear to leave it empty of meaning. One goes over its blankness again and again in one's mind, until one begins to see in it the hand of some occult power punishing one's spiritual pride, or one's shortcomings as a parent. A terrible conclusion to reach about oneself, but at least mere conjunction can now be read as tragedy.

3] This is why some people keep asking themselves if they are happy or not – they feel that happiness would *explain* everything. Unless you can feel that it's all polarized by a general state of happiness, how arbitrary and contingent your muddled little nest of children, money, relations and friends might come to seem!

4] And don't we sometimes work hard to interpret ourselves as unhappy for the same reason? Terrible events occur; how annihilatingly meaningless if I subsequently find myself whistling and thinking of dinner!

5] When we no longer need to run, shoot and endure hardship in order to get our food, then we run for the sake of running, shoot for the sake of shooting, and endure hardship to teach ourselves to endure hardship So, as the question of bare survival recedes, we read for the pleasure of reading. Our interest shifts from what is signified to the process by which we perceive i What lies at the root of our pleasure in pictorial art, says Gombrich, is the tension between what is depicted and the image depicting it – our awareness of the picture as simultaneously marks upon canvas and the subject of those marks. The identity of the murderer, when once we know it, or the message concealed in the cipher, is always a disappointment, a nullity; but the sense that a significance lurks somewhere in that cryptic remark of the victim's widow, that misplaced bottle of paint-stripper, that snatch of a song on the breeze, has kept our mind at full stretch for ten hours or more. If I tell you categorically, as a certain fact, that Bacon wrote Shakespeare, your eyes glaze with boredom. But when you read 'Once more unto the BreACh, dear friends, ONce more'; for the hundredth time, and suddenly see the second, occult, message standing forth in the very flesh of the first, you have for a moment a feeling of revelation, of penetration to the heart of things.

[16] Riddles and puns, metaphor and allegory, religious mysteries, words – with all of them we see one thing, and in that thing another thing.

(An old Ximenes clue: 'Cuckoo-spit on the

Coromandel Coast.' A strange, clear picture comes into one's head of bleached Indian beaches with larval froth crepitating in the sun; then, through it, as one thinks about the ambiguity of 'cuckoo' and 'spit', the picture of a crazy sandbank; and then, when one discovers that a sandbank can be a ras, the crazy sandbank suddenly reveals in its depths the city of Madras.)

7] The Dadaist joke which recurs in art from time to time, of exhibiting a urinal and labelling it 'Urinal', is representation taken to its limiting case, to its extinction in tautology. We look at the urinal, and see in it a urinal. The sudden flat singleness of the operation is a comical reminder of the double vision which we have come to take for granted.

8] The limiting case at the opposite end of the scale (the self-contradiction as opposed to the tautology) is the paradox. Here we are offered an untruth, and are invited to read a truth in it. We leap to see the hidden message, all our sense-seeking faculties challenged by the piquant impossibility of the task. Where the case of self-representation extinguishes sense in nullity, the paradox extinguishes it in universality. Anything, it demonstrates, can be read as anything. 'All goodness is evil,' says a worldly-wise voice. 'There is no white so white as pure blackness.' The mystery, the idea of the whiteness concealed inside the blackness, the new legibility of the blackness, prick our imagination. For a moment we think we see it. But it never becomes clear enough to be banal and obvious, like the identity of the murderer, when once it's known. A general sense of the depth and mystery of things lingers in the air.

[19] Stephen Vizinczey is right: we go into our worst mistakes eyes open, taken with the idea that some marvel must lie concealed beneath their apparent absurdity.

[20] Once one man steadfastly maintains that he can see blackness in the white, or a flying saucer in the sky, others find themselves able to see it as well. They cannot admit, even to themselves, that they lack their neighbour's deep perception beneath the surface of things.

[21] Hidden worlds haunt our imagination. The underworld of criminals; the Underground; the *demi-monde* (occupied in part by the inhabitants of polite society, wearing, as it were, their Hyde aspects).
   The world of the gods; Shangri La; Middle Earth; the world through the Looking-Glass.
   The Mafia; the Establishment; the System; the great conspiracy of the left; the great conspiracy of the right.
   Of these five apparently normal, respectable citizens one is a ruthless murderer who disembowelled Sir Toby with the ornamental Javanese paper-knife!—At

once they all five become deep, interesting in their very uninterestingness.

For fifteen years Mr Hackett lived the life of an ordinary bank manager, in a suburban bungalow at 43 Oakmead Gardens. Now he is unmasked as a Soviet spy. We stare at the pictures of 43 Oakmead Gardens, rivetted by the pebble-dashed walls, the wrought-iron lantern by the front door.

2] *The Truth about . . .* (freemasonry, capitalism, Askenaugh's relations with his secretary, God, supernovae) always turns out to mean a truth lying beneath the surface of things, concealed from you, distorted by interested parties. It's a promise of buried treasure.

23] The most intriguing concealed truths we can be offered are about what lies most plainly in our view. Any editor would hold over *The Truth about the Mafia* (or head-hunters, or the Hapsburgs) for *The Truth about Your Marriage*, or *The Hidden You*.

24] And this is why the forbidden exercises us so much – we feel it's being kept hidden from us. Once we've tasted the apple, and found it tastes just like any other apple, the charm vanishes.

25] No woman so naked as one you can see to be naked underneath her clothes.

[26]   You might think sometimes, looking at novels and plays, that the paradigm of all literature was the Consumers' Association test report. Like electric toasters, the characters of fiction are tested, by stress and crisis, until they break down. And the convention is that what emerges at this point is their 'real' nature, which has up till then remained hidden from others, and often even from the owners of the nature themselves.

It's true that in life people sometimes do surprise us such moments, by revealing flaws or virtues we had not known about before. Because of our fascination with the hidden and its revelation, we are easily persuaded that what emerges is of general rather than particular significance. At last, we feel – with a kind of satisfaction – the truth is emerging! On the surface he has always appeared to be calm and cheerful. But now, after he has spent three days without food, under heavy bombardment, lost his home, and got both shoes full of water, it turns out that *really* – underneath – he is a rather irritable man who lacks the capacity to get pleasure out of life.

We assimilate everything to the extreme cases of Act Five revelation, where people 'break down and confess' that they are murderers, women in disguise, the father of their son's bride. But in most cases the truth that is revealed about us by our behaviour in a crisis is just this: the truth about our behaviour in a crisis.

27] The secret police arrest us all. I, who have been a well-mannered and amusing guest at your dinner parties these past ten years, betray you as soon as they show me the electrodes. That bore Puling refuses, heroically.

If ever we all get out again, don't make the mistake of inviting him to your dinner parties instead of me!

28] There is something a little suspect, anyway, about this general convention that people are not what they seem. The moments of revelation which writers inflict upon their characters rarely reveal, in sophisticated literature, that things are better than had been hitherto supposed. The revelation is nearly always of a disagreeable nature – that the apparently courageous are really cowards, the apparently successful really failures, the apparently happy really miserable; that the apparently meaningful surface of life is really meaningless. The principal aim of some writers seems to be to *put us down*. Are we so up, then, still, after all these years?

29] Of course, in unsophisticated literature things often turn out to be better than they look. Dark clouds have silver linings, cowards summon up their courage, bounders turn up trumps, cads are redeemed by love. Perhaps literature of this sort is intended primarily for people whose lives are hard. The sort of literature where the good is bad underneath is intended for consumption by the privileged classes.

[30] But really, the way we writers knock our characters about! There ought to be a society to protect them. We have them bound, gagged, raped, tortured, shipwrecked and murdered; or, more subtly, condemn them to lead unfulfilled lives and come at last to a realization of their own barrenness and insignificance. I myself have stood by while my own characters were subjected to the most ridiculous humiliations. They're our herd of swine. We cast out all our devils into them, and then ritually destroy them. An infantile procedure, like children smacking their dolls for naughtiness.

I solemnly resolve to show myself in a better light by writing a novel in which the hero comes to realize how significant and fruitful he is, and how solid and substantial are his worldly position and possessions. Various characters who try to suggest otherwise will end up being slowly tortured to death by the excruciating awareness of their own mean-mindedness.

[31] Some writers use, instead of (or as well as) the convention of revelation by crisis, the convention of revelation by pathology. Tired of telling us that we are painfully unextraordinary, they begin to shout instead, 'You're mad! You're sick!' And the paradox catches our imagination. Beneath the surface of our manifest sanity we catch glimpses of swirling disorder

waiting its chance to break out. We feel intimations of a beast within, that may at any moment cast off the skin of good manners and thoughtfulness, and astonish the quiet neighbourhood. For a moment we seem to ourselves agreeably deeper than we thought. Because it *is* to the sane and the well-behaved that these writers address themselves, not to those who have been certified as mad, not to those who have been found guilty of rape and murder.

32] Another way we discomfit our readers: we tell them that the life they lead (life in modern industrial society, life in the world at large today) is false, unnatural, superficial; doesn't, as we imply, achieve some quality accessible to ourselves.

The sort of life that meets our specification, we have told our readers at various times, is lived only among the aristocracy; only among the upper middle class; only by writers; only by the working class (the agricultural working class, the Victorian working class, the Northern working class); only by drug-addicts; only by ourselves and our friends.

No longer possessing the means to sustain any convincing social snobbery, we have branched out into moral snobbery instead.

Novelists, critics, and popularizing psychologists have joined forces to help the laity towards more 'meaningful' relationships and more 'valuable' insights into themselves, towards 'realizing their full potential as human beings'. We shake our heads sadly at people's spiritual poverty, and, smiling kindly, hold out our hands to help them into better ways. We outdo the most sanctimonious of Victorian clergymen. Indeed, some theological writers have been forced to catch up with us, and break into the new secular sanctimony by suggesting that religion is 'about excellence'.

[33] Why do people take hallucinogenic drugs? To see the pretty pictures? Not at all. It's to expand their consciousness. To achieve understanding. To deepen their insights.

In a word, to improve their minds, as if they were going off to a lecture (illustrated with slides) on the folk customs of Basutoland.

[34] A marriage guidance counsellor relates in a Sunday newspaper article how he helps the estranged husband to reassess his behaviour, so that the man cries out in a moment of self-understanding, 'It was *my* fault all the time!' Later, perhaps, if he's really skilled at his job, he gets the wife to realize, in another thunderclap of self-knowledge, that it's all *her* fault.

They may both be right. In any case, it may be necessary to get one's client to acknowledge responsibility if he is ever to be able to do anything about improving the situation. All the same, the truth *might* be just the opposite. If anything in these situations can ever truly be said to be anybody's fault, the correct insight might be, 'It's *her* fault, just like I said it was all the time!'

But insights of this nature would not be encouraged by marriage guidance counsellors.

35] Facing up to one's own goodness – this might be a real moral problem.

36] Opacity has its place, though. Foreigners seem more solid than our own countrymen, more adapted to society, smoother – because we see their external surfaces and nothing else. With our own countrymen we look right through the skin to catch a glimpse of all the knobby social discrepancies and private aspirations within. It is easier to see foreigners (or even members of another social group) as good, or bad, or handsome.

And when you come across someone entirely transparent, someone entirely frank, sincere, undevious, and uncomplicated, it's difficult to feel you ever *know* him. To convince yourself that you know someone you have first to go through a process of getting to know him, of penetrating beneath his surface to something not entirely obvious.

(As a gift is given value by being wrapped, and then unwrapped; as a child is persuaded to want a toy by its being hidden.)

37] We read virtues into ourselves, too, where none exists. We see strength in ourselves where others see nothing but weakness, and put so much effort into maintaining this difficult vision that we become virtuous and strong. The most original thinking is often done by men who have to struggle to understand *anything*. A sense that some huge shape lurks among all that fog draws them on.

[38] Faith, when you think about it, is an odd form of cognition for the religious to lay claim to. In normal usage you *know* what is certain, and believe, or have faith in, only the uncertain. But 'faith' is right. Religious propositions become so hackneyed that you forget the spirit in which they must have been first offered. They were surely deliberate paradoxes, fantasies, crazy fictions, whose deep appeal lay in their very paradoxicality, their very fictitiousness. This is what latter-day religious apologists don't understand. They try to make these radiant absurdities sound *reasonable*.

[39] Metaphysicians, religious zealots and charismatic politicians are like tellers of tall stories who begin, 'You won't believe this, but . . .' They know that nothing is better calculated to induce belief than the challenge of incredibility.

[40] What political and religious enthusiasts have to believe is that the whole tenor and character of human history and human nature may be about to change.

There are no precedents at all for what they expect to see.

[41] Even people of the deepest and most instinctive moderation nourish a secret belief that post-revolutionary societies may have some kind of unique virtue – a certain intangible dignity, perhaps. (They sometimes manifest this belief by their desire to read, over and over again, that it's *not* true.) They cannot quite manage to accept that all the bloodshed and cheering and lies have led to nothing but certain improvements in education and the welfare services. In the same way even the most naturally religionless people cannot quite give up the feeling that there must be . . . *something* above and beyond it all, and . . . *something* after it all. We cling privately to the secret belief that it may be possible to change everything. (As in those dreams where you see someone who has died, and realize it was all only a misunderstanding after all. In dreams everything can be changed and put right. We trail this sweet consoling perfume on with us into the waking world.)

[42] What deeply affects every aspect of a man's experience of the world is his perception that *things could be otherwise*. Look around you now. Without a conscious effort to remain passive you at once begin to formulate attitudes to what you see. You take pleasure in it; you are irritated by it. It could be worse; it could be better.

Among all that never quite complete order, potentialities for greater order continually present themselves to the mind. Your view isn't simple – isn't, as one might say, entirely in the indicative mood. A shifting complex of subjunctives makes it difficult to catch. You don't merely see what is the case. You read into it what might have been the case, and what might yet be the case.

[43]   Imagine a people who lacked this sense that things could be otherwise. Their verbs have no subjunctive, no conditional. A passive folk, we quickly see, not given to discovery, invention or reform. Incapable, too, of judgment or opinion. What happens to them, happens. What will happen, will happen.

They have no regrets, no remorse.

They can feel pain, but not sadness. To be sad is to know that things might have been better.

The pleasure centres of their brains can be stimulated, but they don't know what happiness is. To be happy is to know that things are better than they might be.

(Happiness and sadness are more sophisticated enterprises than we like to allow.)

[44]   One might say that to know what is the case, in any meaningful sense, one must also have some idea in one's head of what is *not* the case, of what it is that one is excluding. To know that Britain is a monarchy, or

that one has five fingers on each hand, one must have some notion that a state can also be a republic, that there are collections of things greater and smaller than five.

'Britain is Britain.' At this point, as the brilliance of the positive meaning slips away into tautology, into nothingness, like the eclipsed sun behind the moon, only the faintly glowing corona of negative meanings is left behind; a hazy cloud of exluded possibilities in which Britons are seen to be gesticulating excitedly, perhaps, and voting Communist.

5] You want your philosophers to amaze you, too. But respectable philosophers insist that their task is to remind you of what you know, buried as it so often is beneath what you have been persuaded to believe.

6] I recognize, with mixed feelings, the conservative nature of this programme. The appeal to knowledge is the appeal to what is the case. The appeal to faith opens up worlds which are not the case. By asserting that they *are* the case it involves us in creating them. We correct reality to suit our vision of it. Sometimes we partially succeed.

We are exhilarated by our self-deception. By the time we have half-altered things to make them fit, the exhilaration has turned to revulsion, and we stop. The world is full of half-realized fantasies.

[47]   The first proposition of the *Tractatus Logico-Philosophicus* – 'The world is everything that is the case' – is the consummation of the empirical tradition in philosophy. The *Tractatus Radico-Philosophicus*, when it comes to be written, will commence: 'The world is everything that might be made to be the case.'

[48]   Each of us develops a style – another attempt to order the chaos. Not by discovering an order in it, but by imposing one upon it, like a tank laying its own tracks across the wilderness. A man dominates his environment by establishing a unifying principle – himself.

[49]   The most plausible styles are pessimistic (tragic, comic, sceptical, cynical). Expecting the worst is a miserable way of spending your life, but you may be able to retain an impassivity in the face of events you can't control which will pass as a sort of kingdom over them. To comport yourself from the very start of the game like a good loser gives you two out of two winning chances.

[50]   Aren't the life-styles which particularly engage us, which give rise to whole ranges of legends and stories, based upon our taste for paradox, our urge to read black in white? Think of the heroes of chivalry, who die to honour a lady's passing whim; the heroes of the imperial ethic, who die rather than disobey an

obviously mistaken order; the members of the *Korporation* who do not flinch as the sword cuts into their faces; the aristocrats who would die rather than make an unmannerly gesture; the addicts who will suffer anything later to enjoy pleasure now. At different times the styles of all these models have seemed deep to us; have held our gaze, made us peer into their smoky depths; made us ponder and sigh, and shake our heads wonderingly; brought lumps to our throats; supported, apparently adequately, the baroque convolutions of extraordinary plots.

] Our ethics, too, end in paradox. The ultimate aims to which we sacrifice our immediate interests get more and more remote, more lost in the clouds, the higher we go – until at last they cease to exist altogether. We place the highest value of all upon the action of someone who sacrifices his life for the sake of another. Isn't what makes such a sacrifice seem so deep to us the sheer lack of any possible justification, the total absence of any return to the martyr, the mind-numbing contrariness of it? Up to that point our sacrifices can be seen as serving some personal goal, however remote, however abstract. At the very least they tend to improve the world in which those who perform them are going to live. But to lay down *one's life*! To make all return of any sort whatsoever impossible! In such total blackness there *must* be light! Light that we cannot see because its brightness blinds us.

[52] 'If not entirely satisfied, just send it back, and we will refund full purchase price.'

The advertisers must feel fairly safe when they mak offers like this. Presumably people don't often send their encyclopedias back, once they've seen them on their shelves, glowing richly in the lamplight.

With a similar escape-clause at the back of our min we are tempted into trying out new opinions, new attitudes, new styles of life. But once we've got used t seeing the beard on our face, and once our friends hav got used to it, it's not so easy to shave it off again.

Tentatively – as a joke, because it's spring – the oak sapling throws out small shoots all over the place without a second thought. But in time the tree has to follow in all seriousness these paths which it has laid down for its own development, growing massively int their capriciousness, and so taking on the fantastic gnarled shape of its maturity.

[53] 'I hate him!' you cry dramatically. And then you begi to hate him.

'I can't live without her!' And then you start to mak mess of your life.

'The whole fabric of society is rotten! We must des everything that stands in our path!' – All right, here's a gun, here's the explosive . . . And you find yourself really going out and blowing up a shop or two.

[54] A toy car is a projection of a real car, made small enough for a child's hand and imagination to grasp.

A real car is a projection of a toy car, made large enough for an adult's hand and imagination to grasp.

5] It seems logical to suppose that fantasy is a projection of reality. But often one can't help feeling that it's the other way round, with the reality breaking surface as an extension of the fantasy within. The people around us are like mountain-tops rising from a sea of cloud.

A lot of our behaviour is like the crimes committed by the insane, where the eruption of the delusion (the rage, the obsession) into the external world often seems arbitrary, almost accidental. It might have been you he killed, and it might have been me; it just happened that it was another person who walked into the house at that particular moment. It just happened that *anyone* walked in.

Sometimes the internal dialogue which goes on inside all men overflows; their lips move, and they smile bitterly to themselves. So with the fantasy murders being committed inside the madman's head. Suddenly an arm is thrown up, a hatchet grasped in the hand. The violence is not so much committed as muttered.

] Each child in the game pursues its individual fantasy. To some extent the roles they are playing are part of the same drama; to some extent not. But this discrepancy they scarcely notice, each being intent upon the subjective experience of his own fantasy rather than its objective effect on others.

[57]   Why do we always want what we haven't got?

You might equally well ask, wouldn't it be more convenient if we were hungry for the last meal instead of the next one?

As soon as we've taken the shining jewel from the s[...] its lustre dries, and it looks much like the pebbles beneath our feet. And we're dismayed at ourselves, as if the jewel might have had some real objective value which our desire for it had merely reflected.

But the real value is our desire. The jewel was only counter in the game. Would it be better if it were the other way about?

You ask (with your admirable high-mindedness) if [...] shouldn't be happier by rising above desire. You aspire to suppress your appetites and longings, and to li[...] in a state of harmonious communion with the univers[...]

So this is *your* desire. This is what *you* want that yo[...] haven't got.

[58]   The objects around us are the typeface in which we s[...] printed deeper messages, stories centering on ourselve[...] as hero, martyr, appetite. It takes a special eye to look at a page of type and see not cherubim and seraphim, but serifs and spacing. It needs a no less conscious detachment to see the naturalistic world naturalistical[...] – without being exhilarated by combinations of sunlight and foliage, crushed by cloud and tar-macadam, flattered or contemptuous at the invitation of certain metropolitan interiors.

And *we* are complex. Complex in ourselves; complex
in our relations with the universe; complex in regard
to each other. This complexity is not merely one of our
qualities – it is fundamental to our nature.

Our consciousness is our complexity manifesting itself.

Our sense of ourselves as subject among objects is our
capacity to perceive our own perceiving, to understand
our own understanding.

What do we have in our brains to differentiate us from
dogs? From snails? From the machines we have built?
From the vastly more sophisticated machines that we
shall build? Only one thing: more.

More; and that more complexly, more subtly,
interconnected.

We think of a dog as having consciousness in some
sense – consciousness of pain, for instance. We can't
imagine any machine that we'd want to say was
conscious of pain. Is that just because we still can't
imagine a machine which is anything like as
complicated as a dog?

We go on adding cells to our machine, interconnecting
circuits. Now it howls when we kick it . . . now it
struggles to get away . . . flinches at the sight of a
raised boot . . . works twice as hard as before . . .

Should we really believe it felt pain? We shouldn't
know *what* to believe. We'd keep insisting that you
could explain it all behaviouristically, without any
recourse to the idea of sensations at all. But we'd feel,

too, that the situation was getting too deep for us.
And we'd hesitate before we kicked it again.

[61] Suppose a computer prints out this: 'I think, therefore
I am.'
    We smile. But its logic is surely no worse than
Descartes's. Seriously! Descartes wasn't making any
claims about the quality of his thought. He was
claiming that any piece of thought-thinking necessarily
implies the existence of a thinker, any piece of
statement-making the existence of a statement-maker.
    – But the computer couldn't *feel* the force of this
necessity!
    – Logical necessity doesn't have to be felt.
    We don't know now whether to smile or click our
tongues in irritation. We rely on computers not to
puzzle us like this.

[62] Our complexity is such that we can understand many
complex things. But not our own complexity!

[63] A capacious suitcase. We can get everything we want
in it: clothes, books, a folding table, a bed, a bicycle .
This suitcase is infinitely flexible! The only thing we
can't get in is the suitcase itself.

[64] We cannot think about our own thinking without
simplification, any more than we can about the world
around us.

We become aware of ourselves in the same way as we do of everything else – by placing (as it were) a construction upon ourselves.

5] Predictivity in all the disciplines which attempt to make a science of human nature and human behaviour is notoriously low. We are too complex, this is the trouble – too complex to be pinned down by creatures no more complex than ourselves.

(Imagine how immeasurably more complicated the study of nuclear particles would become if they had just one human attribute: the ability to read books on particle theory, and to modify their behaviour as a result!)

6] Fashions in reductionism come and go. Now it's animal behaviour. 'Really our aggressive feelings are only the residue of our territorial defence mechanism . . . really smoking is only a displacement activity . . . really we can give a complete explanation of such-and-such behaviour by reference to the triumph ceremony of geese . . .'

We like to put each other down. We like to put ourselves down. Life is easier if we can talk ourselves out of our pretensions, and our intimations of complexity.

7] In some moods, at any rate, it seems to us that Robinson Crusoe is the human archetype. Just as philosophers thought that the thick stew of human discourse, with all its lumpy inaccuracies and indigestible assumptions, could in theory be refined down to pure white crystals – atomic propositions embodying atomic fragments of experience – so we feel that human society, with all its compromises and relativities, is a construction from the series of atomic individuals, each of them sovereign and entire unto himself. We feel that we are Crusoes who happen to have been set down in sight of each other, so that the difficulties of communication and co-operation have been *added* to those of our isolation. As if we are what we are, and *then* we enter into relations with the peopl around us.

But man is the child of men. He comes from the be of another human creature, seeded there by a third. He can become conscious of his thoughts and feelings only by articulating them in a language developed by communication with his fellows. Even in his inmost nature he is defined by his interaction with other beings around him.

What characteristic do we have that can be expresse without relation to others? You are fair-haired, five foot ten, and highly sceptical about everything I'm saying. But only in a world where others are dark-haired, and five foot nine, and also sceptical about things (or less sceptical, or more sceptical!). You are independent of everyone – even completely introverte But only if there are others to be independent of, and introverted from! You dress as you please, without regard to anyone. But what significance does your free choice of clothes have, except in comparison with the choices other people make? You struggle with yourself to fast and pray. But fasting and prayer, in a society where everyone fasts and prays, might purify the spirit no more than polishing your shoes in a society where everyone has shining toecaps.

Crusoe on his island would have been neither brave nor resourceful, neither determined nor ingenious, if he had not come from the society of men; if there were not other men across the sea; if there were not a man to tell the story and men to hear it.

58] You might object that a man is sufficiently complex to be his own social environment. He can be brave because he is braver today than he was yesterday. He can exceed his own expectations, and carry on a conversation with himself. Even in propitious circumstances, one usually numbers oneself among one's audience, among one's critics and sympathizers. But this is an extension of one's social behaviour. No one would – no one *could* – talk to himself without having talked to someone else first.

59] Without any environment at all a man would be nothing – an entity without definition, without dimensions, without outer surfaces. Shut up in the dark, with nothing to see or hear or feel, the psychologist's subjects hallucinate environments for themselves.

Perhaps we dream because we cannot stand the solitude of sleep.

It's fear of this lack of definition that worries us in certain forms of loneliness. We no longer know whether we are good or bad. We feel formless, like heaps of sand that will gradually slide down and disappear into the landscape.

[70] Now let all of us who are moderate, reasonable, fair-minded, balanced and normal, lift up our voices and give thanks to all those who are immoderate, unreasonable, bloody-minded, unbalanced and crazy; because without them as our context it is we who should be the abnormal ones.

If all the 3,500 million people in the world who are more despicable than you were taken out and shot for their shortcomings, you would be the most despicable creature on the face of the earth.

[71] To be good is to be better than.

(Better than in other cases, better than what was the case, better than what might be the case.)

God's Infinite and Perfect Goodness in His Infinite and Perfect Betterness Than.

Than He was last year? This seems theologically unsound. Than He might be? This is trivial. Than us? Yes, than us. Better than you, hypocrite and sinner. Better than me, with my few small lovable faults.

Even with capital letters, these claims sound suddenly rather moderate.

72] You've won? Then I've lost.
Now I've won. And you've lost.
Can't we co-operate, and share first prize? Let's do that. Now *he's* lost.

73] For any to win, some must lose. For any to win significantly, many must lose significantly.
Losing is the contribution which even the poorest and least capable can make towards the common good.

74] Who whom? As Lenin said.
Who rules whom?
Who hands out the soup to whom?
Who is a better person than whom?
Who is more democratic than whom?
Who says 'Who whom?' to whom?

75] And the first shall be last, and the last shall be first. Blessed are the meek: for they shall inherit the earth.
We revised the rules halfway through. Didn't you know? It was a *slow* bicycle race.

76] But I propose that there shall be no more bicycle races, neither slow nor fast; no more winning and losing; no more better and worse; no more who and no more whom!
All those in favour . . .? Carried unanimously.

Now, for anyone who slips back into the old way of thinking I propose a system of re-education and re-indoctrination, backed up if necessary by compulsory labour in the common good . . .

[77] Or else: a society so complex, with so many different struggles going on simultaneously, so many different criteria and ideals and norms and sets of rules, so many different ways of discomfiting the ostensible winners and exalting the losers, that everyone is winning *some* game.

3,500 million games.
3,500 million whos.

[78] We are all brothers!
And with the great warmth of that solidarity running in our veins, we laugh with joy at the sight of each other, and share out the last of our food, and drive out the oppressors who have denied us our brotherhood.

So now we really *are* all brothers. We are all bound to each other with that special closeness that brothers have. That's to say, we are closer to each other than to anyone else.

But now there *is* no one else.

The warmth in our veins begins to cool . . .

Until we notice that some of the brothers are less brotherly than others. With almost as strong a feeling of solidarity as before, we turn on them.

And when they have gone it appears that there are other enemies, within and without. There is always someone against whom our solidarity is expressed.

So that the last embers of that bright warmth don't finally die down until quite far on into the night.

79] Brotherhood, solidarity, unity, love: they all mean these but not those, you but not them.

80] A man makes his arrangements.

81] And his arrangements make the man.

82] Society specifies paradigm arrangements in various fields (marital, financial, emotional, professional, and so on). And some of the sets of arrangements which we assemble around ourselves do actually approximate to these patterns. But our arrangements reflect the complexity of ourselves and of our place in the universe – they can't be captured in a set of patterns any more than the world we see can be described in our notation.

83] We're all 'interested in bondage'.

We cry to be free. Sometimes we mean it, and attempt to free ourselves. But usually it sounds more like the masochist's scream of pain. Not that the pain is unreal, or the scream insincere. Probably the client who has had himself tied up howls to be released, too – even struggles to get out of his bonds, chokes with claustrophobia, repents of the whole idea. He suffers, all right; then makes a date for the next session.

[84]   'What do we want? Everything! When do we want it?
       Now!'
            What do we really want? The pleasure of shouting,
       'What do we want? Everything . . .'
            And when do we want it? – We've got it already.

[85]   The *sense* of liberty is a message read between the lines
       of constraint. Real liberty is as transparent, as
       odourless and tasteless, as water.

[86]   But why do people think that political freedom is
       somehow *natural*? That it comes bubbling up like
       springwater as soon as you break the constraints on
       which society is based? Political liberty is a highly
       sophisticated and fragile structure. You think of
       'society', and it's so large and vague that you can
       believe almost anything of it. But think of two people
       sharing a room – two friends, even two lovers – and
       you see at once that they must behave with the
       greatest thoughtfulness and skill if they are both to
       feel unrestricted in their occupation of the room. Now
       think of *three* people sharing a room . . .

[87]   What do we do with freedom when we get it? Why, we
       press it at once to the point where it impinges upon the
       freedom of others, so that they are forced to react and
       restrict our new freedom.
            Then we cry, 'See, it wasn't real freedom after all!'

A happy sound; our comfortably worn leg-shackle has been restored to us, and we can sit at home just like we used to.

8] 'We are all free. We cannot be compelled. We can always choose suffering or death rather than submit, and to pretend otherwise is *mauvaise foi*. The slave acquiesces in his slavery.'

And suddenly it all looks simple, in an agonizing way – as simple, and as agonizing, as it does if you take the converse view that nothing is anyone's responsibility. A moment's thought, however, and it doesn't seem all that simple after all. We are free to die rather than (let's say) cause suffering to another human being. Free to die rather than see him suffer a cut finger? Yes, but we don't mean that! What do we mean? Two cut fingers? This is being foolish. Two *broken* fingers? Three broken fingers and a ruptured spleen?

Mathematics seems out of place here. When we talk about our freedom like this, we are not in the realms of description (as it at first might seem) but of exhortation. Death before dishonour!

Brave words. But we are also free to let others suffer rather than to submit. I have the freedom to watch five hostages shot rather than myself reveal the password, or accept conversion. I have this freedom. I may exercise it. But, put like this, my freedom not to submit sounds less glorious.

[89] Certainly, to be compelled is not to be worked like a puppet. To be compelled is to recognize that one must act against one's wishes in one respect in order to secure some other objective. And some other objective can always be found. The only man who cannot be compelled is one who is indifferent not just to his own fate, but to *everyone's* fate.

[90] You might say that this is just what ethically interesting behaviour is: forgoing short-term objectives to secure long-term ones, or one's own interests to secure other people's.

Philosophers have talked themselves into a weird state of puzzlement over ethics. They have professed themselves unable to see how we could be under any moral obligation to prefer one objective to another unless that objective were itself morally preferable – which is to say that we had a moral obligation to prefer it. 'Ought', they have declared, can never be derived from 'is'.

One would like to reply that it can however be derived perfectly well from 'if'. If you're going to Normandy you ought to try the overnight ferry from Southampton. (I don't know and don't need to know whether you ought to be in Normandy.) If you're going to exterminate any very substantial section of the population you ought (yes, morally ought!) to rise early, and study hard, and refuse all bribes and inducements to use scarce transportation for other

purposes. Your behaviour, as you forgo lunch once
again to keep the trains rolling to the camps, is *moral*
behaviour.

Does there have to be a moral rule that one must put
the interests of others above one's own in order for it
to be admirable to give one's last sip of water to
another? One might as well ask, does there have to be
a rule that pain is against one's interests for it to be
sensible not to put one's hand in the fire?

1] The objectives which our moral behaviour is designed
to secure are not themselves moral. Not in *that*
context, at any rate; they may be moral within some
further terms of reference. They are no more
inherently self-explanatory than any of our other goals.

Sometimes they are so obvious and simple that
(philosophically) we cannot see them because we gaze
right through them, looking for something deep.
Sometimes they are so remote and general that they
have disappeared into the clouds. Asked what they are,
we can no longer clearly answer. We trudge up the
mountain through the mist, guided entirely by the
sheer upwardness of the ground.

2] Imagine a tribe which lived by its precepts completely,
lived by them with chemical purity, as if they were the
laws of chemistry. They explain that, because
obtaining money by false pretences is wrong, money is
not obtained by false pretences. Very moral people,

undoubtedly. And yet one feels that they're not so much moral, as morally inert. Their precepts are stationed in the wrong places – yeomen warders guarding a tower no one wants to attack. The logic of morality involves a tension, if not a contrast, between moral standards and moral practice.

[93] Man is a marvellously sophisticated and effective agent. It's as a principal that his performance is so erratic.

[94] All animals are fundamentally machines for achieving an objective. Their objective is simple and universal: survival. And this objective is built-in. They have evolved as survival-machines because survival-machines tend to survive.

Men have a problem because, in certain sections of certain societies, they have been too successful in achieving this inbuilt objective. They have arranged the world around them so that survival is easy. It occupies only a small proportion of the machine's capacity. Other objectives have to be found, if the machinery is not to run down, or consume itself. Our great cry is what a computer would say, if it were sophisticated enough to understand its problem: 'Programme me!'

So we find objectives for ourselves. We play, like young animals who do not yet have to find their own food. We invent games with whatever happens to surround us – mountains, sea, money, other people.

And after we have played for a while we weary of playing. The objectives we have invented for ourselves, we see, are arbitrary, meaningless, not serious.

5] Our goals are *indefensible*. It is this indefensibility which makes us defend them with such blind violence and intolerance.

We dare not look at them, or think about them. So we keep our backs to them, and fill our minds with rage.

And, often, manoeuvring and staggering in our fight to the death to preserve them, abandon them without even noticing it.

6] Our goals have no inherent goalishness, no natural quality which makes them recognizable as goals. A ball passes between two white posts: there is nothing about this event in itself which makes it self-evidently desirable. It's *made* desirable by the rules of football. It's desirable because the rules of football say it's desirable. It's the conventions of the game which give the goal meaning.

And it's the goal which gives the conventions of the game meaning.

You can have an enjoyable game of football without any goals being scored at all. You can imagine a game so hard-fought in the midfield that no one noticed the posts were being taken down by the bailiffs. It wouldn't matter at all – provided no one noticed.

[97] The goal might be not only conventional but sordid –
the accumulation of wealth, for instance. Or worse
than sordid – the destruction of a human race. And
yet its pursuit might yield happiness. What satisfying
skills one might display, what exhilarating dangers one
might run, on the way from one's second to one's third
million! How honourable and free one would feel,
refusing bribes and spurning threats in order to keep
the trains running to the death camps on time!

[98] One goal, though, whose pursuit is unlikely to yield
happiness is happiness itself.
   'The pursuit of happiness . . .' What a fatal
abbreviation Jefferson made here! A moment's
thought, and you see what he means: the pursuit of
objectives which will yield happiness. But we don't
stop to think. The phrase gives off a metaphysical
glow. It seems to offer a way of by-passing the
objectives, in all their absurdity, of leaping over the
tedious riches, the heavy learning, the stiff codes and
styles of life, and going straight to the source of the
light which they reflect.
   It's as if, enchanted by spacious rooms, we
commissioned the space, without the walls and ceiling
that surround the space. Or, aroused by the sexuality
of women, but discouraged by their menstruation,
their talk, their thoughts, their habit of having
relatives, and their subjectivity, we tried to get the
sexuality without the women themselves. (Which, of
course, we do try to do.)

9] Our trouble is not (as is sometimes supposed) that people in our society are less happy than formerly, or that less people are happy, or that more people are less happy. (Indeed, it's difficult to give much objective meaning to these expressions of unease.) Our trouble is that, because happiness is now so commonly the goal, and because this goal is a chimerical one, more people are conscious of a failure to reach their goal in life.

0] There is a sense, though, in which one can be happy at will. There is a certain latitude in the interpretation of one's own state; the criteria of happiness and unhappiness are not entirely definitive and objective. The definition of a happy man is like the only definition of a Jew which the authors of a book on the Jewish population of Britain could find – a man who, when asked if he was a Jew, said yes.

1] An odd sort of definition, though. At certain expansive moments, having about a third of a pint of Jewish blood in my veins, I like to claim to be a Jew. But only to Gentiles. I haven't yet met a Jew I thought would believe me, whatever the authors of the book said. ('*You* think you're a sea-captain,' as Sam Goldwyn's mother says to him in the joke, when he shows off his new nautical rig to her. '*I* think you're a sea-captain. But would a sea-captain think you're a sea-captain?')

So when you come up to me, your face grey with anxiety, your voice breaking with misery, and tell me you're perfectly happy, I cannot help feeling that you have miscategorized yourself. Through pride, perhaps. Or perhaps through ignorance of what it is to be happy.

And when the people around me, guiltily conscious of their advantages in a hard world, experiment with attitudes of desperation, I feel I'd like to take them by the arm (like a chaplain), and say:

Reflect! You may be happier than you think!

[102] The charm of travelling is that it offers a rare combination of purpose and idleness. We sit back in the driver's seat, or in our chaise-longue on the sun-deck, and relax, reassured by the sensation of moving towards an objective.

[103] And how much of one's life is spent not in being or doing at all, but merely in waiting to be or to do. But waiting, too, is goal-directed – the lowest, and probably the commonest, form of goal-directed activity (or non–activity). One stage lower than travelling.

[104] Much of the overwhelming charm of a love affair is this: that every aspect of it, every word and glance and rendezvous, is polarized by its relation to an objective. In every conversation, in every silence, both parties know which way is forward (and which sideways, and which back).

But even here, in this highly charged, highly polarized situation, the goal is conventional, is given meaning by the conventions of the activity. In certain circumstances a kiss, or even a look, might be the symbol which counted as a goal; in other circumstances, nothing less than the rearrangement of one's entire life-style. Even where the objective is understood to be copulation – which has a self-explanatory air, as the natural terminus of a fundamental animal urge – the act bears a symbolic charge beyond the physical gratification it offers. (Even the most unromantic eroticist finds the prospect of intercourse more compelling than the prospect of masturbation.) These gestures of offering and exposure symbolize submission. Or perhaps 'submission' suggests something too one-sided, and too once-and-for-all. 'Admission' is closer. Lovers offer and seek admission to each other's inward selves, inside the outer surfaces which confront the rest of the world. Once all inward motion has ceased, the love affair ends. Perhaps now the tranquillity of established love reigns and endures (very different from the turbulence of the affair). But neither that security, nor continued physical pleasure, may be enough to insulate the participants against the electric charm of another affair, with another partner.

05] Pascal: 'Aussi les hommes qui sentent naturellement leur condition n'évitent rien tant que le repos: il n'y a rien qu'ils ne fassent pour chercher le trouble . . .

'Ainsi on se prend mal pour les blâmer; leur faute n'est pas en ce qu'ils cherchent le tumulte, s'ils ne le cherchaient que comme un divertissement; mais le mal est qu'ils le recherchent comme si la possession des choses qu'ils recherchent les devait rendre véritablement heureux, et c'est en quoi on a raison d'accuser leur recherche de vanité; de sorte qu'en tout cela et ceux qui blâment et ceux qui sont blâmés n'entendent la véritable nature de l'homme.

'Et ainsi, quand on leur reproche que ce qu'ils recherchent avec tant d'ardeur ne saurait les satisfaire, s'ils répondaient, comme ils devraient le faire s'ils y pensaient bien, qu'ils ne recherchent en cela qu'une occupation violente et impétueuse qui les détourne de penser à soi, et que c'est pour cela qu'ils se proposent un objet attirant qui les charme et les attire avec ardeur, ils laisseraient leurs adversaires sans répartie. Mais ils ne répondent pas cela, parce qu'ils ne se connaissent pas eux-mêmes. Ils ne savent pas que ce n'est que la chasse, et non pas la prise, qu'ils recherchent . . .

'Ils s'imaginent que, s'ils avaient obtenu cette charge, ils se reposeraient ensuite avec plaisir, et ne sentent pas la nature insatiable de leur cupidité. Ils croient chercher sincèrement le repos, et ne cherchent en effet que l'agitation.

'Ils ont un instinct secret qui les porte à chercher le divertissement et l'occupation au dehors, qui vient du ressentiment de leurs misères continuelles; et ils ont un autre instinct secret, qui reste de la grandeur de notre première nature, qui leur fait connâitre que le bonheur n'est en effet que dans le repos, et non pas dans le tumulte; et de ces deux instincts contraires, il se forme en eux un projet confus, qui se cache à leur vue dans le fond de leur âme, qui les porte à tendre au repos par l'agitation, et à se figurer toujours que la satisfaction qu'ils n'ont point leur arrivera, si, en surmontant quelques difficultés qu'ils envisagent, ils peuvent s'ouvrir par là la porte au repos.

'Ainsi s'écoule toute la vie. On cherche le repos en combattant quelques obstacles; et si on les a surmontés, le repos devient insupportable . . .'

[Pascal: 'So men who are by nature aware of their condition avoid nothing so much as repose; there is nothing they would not do to seek out turmoil . . .

'Thus one is wrong to blame them; their fault lies not in their seeking tumult, if they sought it only as a diversion; the trouble is that they seek it as if possession of the things they pursue must indeed make them happy, and it is therein that one is right to brand their quest vain; so that here both those who blame and those who are blamed fail to understand the true nature of man.

'And thus, when they are taxed that what they pursue with such eagerness could not satisfy them, if they replied, as they ought to do if they thought about it aright, that they sought in this only a violent and headlong occupation to distract them from thinking about themselves, and that it was for this reason that they set themselves up an objective which charmed them and drew them eagerly on, they would leave their critics without an answer. But they do not so reply, because they themselves lack self-knowledge. They do not know that it is only the chase and not the prize that they seek . . .

'They imagine that if they had obtained this or that office, they would then gladly rest, and do not feel the insatiable nature of their cupidity. They believe that they sincerely pursue repose, and in fact pursue only turbulence.

'They have a secret instinct, springing from the sense of their unending woes, which leads them to seek diversion and occupation outside themselves; and they have another secret instinct, remaining from the greatness of our primal nature, which makes them aware that happiness is only in repose, and not in tumult; and from these two contrary instincts there takes shape within them a confused scheme, hidden from their sight in the depths of their soul, which leads them to reach for repose by way of turbulence, and ever to imagine that the satisfaction they do not possess will come to them if they can, by overcoming some few difficulties which they foresee, thereby open before them the doorway to repose.

'Thus the whole of life runs past. A man seeks repose by battling against obstacles; and, these surmounted, repose becomes unendurable . . .]

06] The piquancy of this superb piece of observation comes from its brilliant disdain. But how strange this religious disdain of the world is! It suggests that it would be better if the prize were in fact more satisfying than the chase; that human life would be richer and truer if the glass of beer to which one looked forward as one walked did give one a year of satisfaction and repose instead of only ten minutes. Is that what the religious really want to say, that the walk could be nothing and the glass of beer everything? In fact they do. Because they see the whole of life as a walk leading up to the Perfect Glass of Beer, which will keep them in contentment for eternity. Did Pascal not for one instant feel the insatiable nature of his own cupidity as he wrote? Did it not for one second dawn upon him that his description of 'their' belief, that by surmounting certain difficulties they could open the door to repose, was in fact an exact description of the religious life?

Perhaps not; and this is why he is so effective. To be effective one must perceive the vain cupidity in others; but in oneself see nothing but the glitter of the gold.

07] It's surprising how the world – particularly human nature – is often most precisely observed by those who do not like what they see. Perhaps their feelings are more ambiguous than they suppose.

08] We struggle (against our oppressors, against ignorance, against disease, against the faults in ourselves), and in our struggle we are determined, courageous, admirable. We surpass ourselves. So much so that our efforts are crowned in victory. And in victory we have no further opportunity for determination or courage. We cease to be admirable. We fall beneath ourselves. Our virtues are self-abolishing. Our achievements rob us of the possibility of achieving.

[109] The goal of the ambitious young executive is to become Chairman. Does that mean the thirty years on the way up will be validated only by the three in the Chairman's office? The objective of the nation's economic policy is a surplus in the balance of payments. Does that mean that the labour of ten million people, the goods they produce and the food they consume, will be given meaning only by certain figures in a Treasury report next quarter?

Perhaps in cases like these we should speak not of goals and objectives, but of cadences. The dynamic of tonal music comes from its progression towards a cadence, towards its resolution in certain chords. But the cadence is not the point of the music – reaching it is not what the music is *for*. The succession of dominant and tonic is satisfying only because of its context, only because it is the culmination of the structure which leads up to it. We don't go to the theatre to see the hero lying there with a sword in him; we go to see by what complications of structure this inevitable finale will be put off for five acts. You might say that even the simplest and most direct pleasures of life – conversation, making love, going for a walk – all depend upon this elaboration of structure towards a cadence.

10] The animal in us demands satisfaction as soon as the need arises. With increasing sophistication we postpone the cadence further and further – like the couple in the Japanese picture, always referred to with approval in manuals of sexual behaviour, who are taking tea together at a table while coitally engaged below it. There are forms of coitus mentioned in the manuals (though at this point their tolerance fails) where orgasm is never reached at all. In art, too, we try to do without cadences, irritated by their banality, adopting atonal systems where no resolution is possible, abandoning the conventions which make a plot knottable and unknottable. We move higher and higher into the thin air, first exhilarated, then enervated, and longing to get back to animal immediacy.

11] Death is the cadence to life. The structure of life is polarized and given meaning by its culmination in death.

12] This is difficult to keep in mind. We alternate between two converse metaphysical extremes in our view of death. Sometimes we see it as the point of life.

Sometimes we see it as a mockery of life.

All our aspirations and endeavours, we feel in this second mood, are vain because death will put an end to them. This is like saying that a play is futile because eventually it ends. That a play ends, and that life ends, is on the contrary *of the essence*.

[113] After all, life is not static. We change, we develop. Those who wish to abolish death (whether by physical or metaphysical means) – at what stage of life do they want the process to be halted? At the age of twenty? At thirty-five, in our prime? To be thirty-five for two years sounds attractive, certainly. But for three years? A little dull, surely. For five years – ridiculous. For ten – tragic.

The film is so absorbing that we want this bit to go on and on . . .

You mean, you want the projector stopped, to watch single motionless frame? No, no, no, but . . . Perhaps you'd like the whole sequence made up as an endless band, and projected indefinitely? Not that, either.

The sea and the stars and the wastes of the desert go on forever, and will not die. But the sea and the stars and the wastes of the desert are dead already.

[114] There is nothing that enriches life as much as the certainty of death.

The intense sweetness of music, of summer, of pleasure in love, is that they are *already passing*, almost before we can take them in. This moment has gone, now this, now *this* . . . Our sense of their preciousness turns upon our ever-present sense of loss. Only in spending and losing can value be realized. Hoarded gold is an abstraction, inert, a miser's dream.

It is a condition of total Romantic love that it is doomed; only the certainty that it will end makes such blind unreasoning commitment possible. In the same way our mortality is the condition of life's painful sweetness.

15] And yet the cruelty of that condition is more than we can bear.

16] 'Death,' says Wittgenstein in the *Tractatus*, 'is not an event in life; we do not live to experience death.'

Death (as he might have said) is the limiting case of life's experiences. It defines them by standing just outside them, as the tautology does the calculus of meaningful propositions, in Wittgenstein's usage.

17] How the solidity and absoluteness of the limiting case fascinate us! It monopolizes our attention to the point where it begins to seem *normative*. Philosophers in the past became fixated upon the tautology as the standard to which all propositions had to aspire, as if our entire discourse consisted in failed tautologies. We're like prisoners who become obsessed with the walls around the exercise-yard, or plainsmen who think that the mountains on the horizon are the real world.

[118]   The limiting case limits not like an ordinary fence but
        like an electrified one. It stands immediately outside
        the zone it defines; the range of movement it prescribe
        extends up to it, but not into contact with it.

[119]   But still we fling ourselves upon the wire.
        We find some of our experience delusory, some of our
        knowledge open to doubt; we can devise no absolute
        certain-sure test to protect ourselves against the
        possibility of finding this kind of mistake inside
        ourselves; and we run headlong for the safety of the
        absolute. *All* our experience is delusory, we cry, with
        deep masochistic satisfaction, *all* our knowledge is
        dubious. In just such a way, says Max Black, we could
        anxiously screw the criteria for colour-blindness
        tighter and tighter until we had shown that everyone
        was colour-blind. But at this point we should have
        ceased to make any statement about the world.
        Because the function of saying that some people are
        colour-blind is to distinguish between the capabilities
        of different people. When we say that really everyone
        is colour-blind, or that really all our experience is an
        illusion, we're not breaking through to some ultimate
        truth about the universe, we're simply removing the
        concepts of colour-blindness and illusion from our
        vocabulary. We're not protecting ourselves against the
        contingency of the world, we're leaving ourselves more
        vulnerable than ever.
            All this is a philosophical commonplace. But we nee

it by us at all times to protect us against the facile despair which we are so repeatedly offered. Once a week the astonished cry goes up that all happiness is false, all love self-seeking, all goodness insincere. Once a month we say it to ourselves.

And we need it, too, against enthusiasms of the opposite sort. Against claims that everything is evidence of God's mercy, against assertions of universal love and universal brotherhood. If we live in a world where we can all love each other, and all be brothers, and where cancer is a manifestation of God's inscrutable mercy, then we live in a world where love, brotherhood, and mercy do not exist.

b]   Eternal ecstasy!
     Perpetual adoration!
     An unwavering intensity of love!
     One might as well say a permanent orgasm. And even the most unreflecting sexualist would see that there was some fundamental misunderstanding here.

– Why? Can't you imagine (in another world, after the revolution) that moment of utter self-dissolution being (as it were) the one long moment of eternity?

– I cannot. It is in the very inmost nature of all these exaltations that they exalt, bear one up, alter one's state.

– Very well; throughout eternity one journeys up and up, endlessly higher and higher . . .

– What? Without climax, without achievement, without release?

These exaltations, these epiphanies, are events in ti
which begin, and run their course, and cease (if only t
begin again).

So is happiness, and even contentment. What woul
mean, to be happy, if one had never been unhappy, if
one might not be unhappy again? To be happy is to t
happier than. Eternal happiness is the limiting case –
the tautology, the universal colour-blindness.

And yet myths of eternal happiness haunt us. Look
soberly at the future, we secretly but seriously expect
it to consist of a more or less unwavering happiness.

At least, we optimists do, on Saturdays, in early
summer, and on calm afternoons at the beginning of
November.

[121] Not that we should put it like that, of course – 'eterna
life', 'eternal happiness'. All we want, we practical
men, is just a little more than we have.

But as in a similar formula in mathematics (after an
one, another one), infinity is already generated and
expressed.

[122] The amusements of our youth amuse us no longer
when we are old; the diversions of health and life
cease to divert when we are sick and faced with death
So, we conclude, with another of our fearful pieces of
retroactive legislation, those amusements and
diversions must always have been futile, shallow, and
false. We make sickness and death the standards.

I recover from a severe illness, but cannot lose my

sense of the futility of human amusements. Now, I solemnly inform you, I see into the depths of things, I see how things really stand. It's as if, having had my legs amputated, I began to insist that I never had really walked, that nobody had ever walked, that walking was an illusion.

If making love, or making money, or playing cards, amuse us even for only an hour, then for that hour they amuse us, and no subsequent experience, no subsequent revelation, no subsequent alteration of our perception, can change that.

] I can't help feeling that one can detect a secret belief in *progress* here, even among those who would disavow the idea most vehemently. 'One comes to see the futility of human pleasures.' Behind this is the assumption that one becomes wiser as time goes on, that one's later view of things is more valid than one's earlier view simply because it is later. The same phenomenon can be shown from the opposite angle: 'One loses the ability to appreciate human pleasures.' Now one sees the finger pointed at the observer instead of the observed; one sees his change of attitude take its sad place with his failing eyesight and impaired hearing.

Supposing, after all, the wise old man said, 'I understand now the true blurredness and inaudibility of things.'

Now we see a golden city in the clouds; now we do not. We do not grow wiser or more percipient at the moment we lose sight of it.

[124] Pascal: 'Nous ne nous tenons jamais au temps présent.
Nous anticipons l'avenir comme trop lent à venir,
comme pour hâter son cours; ou nous rappelons le
passé pour l'arrêter comme trop prompt: si
imprudents, que nous errons dans les temps qui ne
sont pas nôtres, et ne pensons point au seul qui nous
appartient; et si vains, que nous songeons à ceux
qui ne sont plus rien, et échappons sans réflexion le
seul qui subsiste. C'est que le présent, d'ordinaire,
nous blesse. Nous le cachons à notre vue, parce qu'il
nous afflige; et s'il nous est agréable, nous regrettons
de le voir échapper. Nous tâchons de le soutenir par
l'avenir, et pensons à disposer les choses qui ne sont
pas en notre puissance, pour un temps où nous
n'avons aucune assurance d'arriver.

'Que chacun examine ses pensées, il les trouvera
toutes occupées au passé et à l'avenir. Nous ne pensons
presque point au présent; et, si nous y pensons, ce
n'est que pour en prendre la lumière pour disposer de
l'avenir. Le présent n'est jamais notre fin: le passé et
le présent sont nos moyens; le seul avenir est notre fin.
Ainsi nous ne vivons jamais, mais nous espérons de
vivre; et, nous disposant toujours à être heureux, il est
inévitable que nous ne le soyons jamais.'

[Pascal: 'We never remain in the present. We anticipate
the future as being too slow to come, as if to hasten its
progress; or we recall the past in order to hold it back
as being too quick to go: we are so rash as to stray into

times which are not ours, and do not think about the only one which belongs to us; so futile as to think of those which no longer are, and to let slip unreflecting the only one which subsists. The truth is that the present commonly wounds us. We hide it from our sight, because it distresses us; and if we find it agreeable, we are sorry to see it escape. We strive to endure it by means of the future, and think to arrange things which are not within our power, against a time that we have no assurance of reaching.

'Let each of us examine his thoughts, and he will find them all taken up with the past and with the future. About the present we think scarcely at all; and if we do, it is only to use its light to command the future. The present is never our end: the past and the present are our means; the future alone is our end. Thus we never live, but hope to live; and, ever disposing ourselves to be happy, inevitably never are.']

5] It's true, we don't live in the present. What stops us? Some kind of universal character defect? (Suspect all allegations of universal defects!) Or is the present strictly speaking uninhabitable?

I think of the moments in my life that came closest to living-in-the-present, moments of experience so intense, when I was so involved in a game, so taken up with formulating a difficult thought, so overwhelmed by a physical pleasure, that I really wasn't reliving what happened the day before, or imagining what would happen the day after. (It's moments of absorption like these that in other, metaphysical moments we aspire to recapture and make permanent.) But when I examine these experiences more finely my suspicions are aroused. Was my absorption in the game, or the thought, not entirely dependent upon my consciousness of the situation as a developing one? Upon my awareness that the ball had been there, and would go *there* if I struck it so? Upon my feeling that the words in my head were on the way to expressing some sense already glimpsed? And even physical pleasure, which at first sight seems so immediate and self-contained, depends intimately upon a consciousness of the past, and an anticipation of the future; upon recognition and alteration; upon a sense of security or a sense of impermanence; upon some continuing structure of relationships with things or with others. Without a context, the very same electric current in the very same nerve might be a pain instead of a pleasure. Or pass unnoticed.

[126] But even this, one might insist, begs the question. To feel these contextual complexities is to consider one's consciousness over an extended period of time, the end of which must lie in the future when one enters upon it, and the beginning of which must already be in the past by the time one has completed it. When I talk about living in the present, I'm referring to my experience just precisely *now*.

Ah, *now*! That odd time – the oddest of all times; the time it always is. There really shouldn't be any mystery about it, since we've had such an opportunity to study the period. And yet, by the time we've reached the 'w' of 'now' the 'n' is ancient history, buried in the past as surely as the reign of Nebuchadnezzar and the fall of Troy, with the ray of light that flashed from my tooth as I said it already almost halfway to the moon.

But at each moment as I ploughed through 'now' it was now. It could be depicted as an advancing line behind which the sound-waves appeared. A mathematical line, without width?

Exactly; the line of division between past and future. So the past extends up to the very point where the future begins? Of course! – In that case, you can't live *in* the present any more than you can live *in* the border between Kent and Sussex. One moment it's Kent and the next it's Sussex – there's nothing between them. That's what being a line is. One moment it's 'will be' and the next it's 'was'. To say something *is* is like saying it's *on* the border; partly in Kent, partly in Sussex – partly was and partly will be.

It's not only *always* now, but *never* now.

7] The present is the limiting case of the past; history taken to the absurd extreme where, like a tautology, it seems to evaporate in our hands.

8] So let each of us examine his thoughts, as Pascal asks. And then, having found them indeed all taken up with the past and future, let's get on with it and enjoy both past and future alike, as our rich and rightful domain. Yesterday she kissed you; tonight you'll see her again. You're a happy man, and I don't imagine you'll let Pascal tell you otherwise.

[129] And now, like a sensible linguistic philosopher, I ask myself how I actually use the word 'now' with such apparent success in everyday conversation. I use it as I'm using it now; you understand it in the way you're now understanding it. This is the function it serves, as the temporal equivalent of 'here', to mean 'at the same time as I utter these words', just as 'here' means 'in the same place that I utter them'. You could make a metaphysical problem out of 'here', too, if you detached it from the context of its use by a particular speaker in a particular place. And you could make another metaphysical problem out of it by demanding increasing exactitude. 'Come here!' I call – and you obediently come to within conversational range. 'No, here!' I insist – and you stand on my toes and crush your stomach against mine. 'You're still not *exactly* where I am!' I complain. You climb into my mouth and squeeze down into my oesophagus. It's no good; can't you understand that when I say *here* I mean occupying exactly the same piece of space as myself, neither more nor less . . .?

30] Unpeople the world experimentally. There will be
nothing to which 'I' and 'you' refer, and no 'here',
either. Will there be a 'now'?

I shift uneasily in my seat at the question, my
imagination floundering. Cautiously, I imagine
processes going forward – planets revolving, radio-
carbon decaying. Various events would be
simultaneous; various processes regular with respect to
each other. At different moments things would have
reached different stages . . .

A guarded statement! But perhaps not guarded
enough. When I mention 'different moments' I'm
already postulating an observer to nominate them.
When I say that certain events are 'simultaneous', I'm
already specifying the possibility of a particular single
point from which they could be observed. Now I don't
know what to say. The idea of earlier and later – the
whole possibility of motion and process – seems to
have collapsed. Am I to imagine a world in which
planets don't revolve, in which radio-carbon doesn't
decay? This seems more observed than ever – a
snapshot of the universe. You might insist that if we
can't have moments without men to nominate them,
then we can't have planets and carbon without men to
name them, either. And I have to concede this. Of an
unpeopled universe one can say nothing, not even that
planets revolve and radio-carbon decays. To speak is to
people the universe.

[131]   But in this unpeopled universe there could still be dogs
        and cats and spiders (let's say), perceiving the
        movements of their prey, the alternation of day and
        night, and various other things of interest to them.
        Can I construct a universe of sorts around *their*
        perception?
            Only in so far as I can imagine myself into their skin.
        They do not say 'I' and 'here' and 'now'. I have to
        imagine myself seeing through their eyes and speaking
        on their behalf.

[132]   This is an unfashionably anthropocentric view of
        things, at a time when well-intentioned men are
        trying to persuade us to take our modest place among
        the animal species, in the last few moments of
        geological time; to see ourselves from a great height as
        a brief and insignificant episode in the history of the
        universe. And we can do this; our ability to project
        ourselves by means of language and imagination is
        dizzying. But it remains true that our language and
        imagination are inherently anthropocentric. Our
        conception of time and space – of the universe which
        we inhabit – cannot be prized loose from human
        experience and made to float on its own.

[133]   'Of an unpeopled world one can say nothing . . .' Is
        this a kind of idealism? – What the idealist says of an
        unperceived world is that it doesn't exist. This is far
        from saying nothing!

34] And now . . . I start to wonder whether this anthropocentric explanation of now hasn't side-stepped the whole issue. It misses – I don't know how to put it – the essential objective element. The point is not that now is when I utter these words, but that when I utter these words is now. It's now *now*, even when I'm not uttering any words. And if it's now for me, it's now for you . . .

Even though I'm in London, and you're in New York? Of course! I'm reading your latest letter, which has taken three days to get here. 'Right now,' you tell me, 'I'm feeling fine . . .' But that was three days ago. Right *now* (as I read your letter) you may be lying stabbed on the sidewalk. Do I mean that I could fly there, as swift as lightning, and see you on the sidewalk? No, I mean more than that. But then I think about developments on Sirius. The light I'm now seeing from Sirius left eight years ago. Anything may be happening there now! Do I mean that I can imagine getting more up-to-date information? But nothing (according to Einsteinian physics, at any rate) can travel faster than light. My notion of things happening there now is a kind of imaginative projection.

35] In an otherwise objective universe our subjectivity is a great and unnatural burden to carry about with us. Compared with ourselves, everything around us is neat, solid, contained. We move among it without definition, transparent, like a cloud of gas.

So we try to objectivize ourselves – to see ourselves fr•
outside as extensions of the natural universe, subject to
its laws and beyond our own control. We look at the
universe, with ourselves standing well-disguised in the
midst of it, and say, as it were with a wry smile, 'So
that's the way things are!'

In this way the religious see themselves as instrumen
of God's will; political fanatics as instruments of the
historical process; and Don Quixote as an instrument
of Dulcinea. We accept with relief the assurances of
psychologists that we are in the grip of occult but
objective forces within – needs, drives, reflexes,
behaviour patterns, compulsions, complexes, and a
hundred other steel springs and brass cog-wheels.

Commenting on our performance with interest and
insight, we explain:

I need this kind of stimulation.

I just have a thing about physical pain.

I don't know *why* I hate her so much; I just know th
I do.

It comes from here. (Indicating the heart.)

It comes from here. (Indicating the gut.)

It's simply an emotional response, that's all.

It's a purely cerebral exercise, nothing more.

And we try to detach our subjective judgments and
interpretations of the world from ourselves. We paste
them to their objects under cover of darkness, and ther
discover them there in the morning, when we draw
back the curtains and stand amazed at a world full of
hatefulness and admirableness.

6] Each time we catch sight of ourselves in a mirror, or in a photograph, we feel a little shock of surprise (and relief). We're still managing to present some kind of objective exterior to the world! We're still managing to pass ourselves off with some plausibility in the world of tables and chairs, of men and women! When you look straight into your eye in the mirror, of course, you never quite convince yourself. But you feel that just possibly you might be able to keep your secret from others.

7] Don't we look at ourselves simply because we're vain? Surely; but this is *why* we're vain. We're trying to establish our objective existence, trying to stake a place in the world of observable and observed phenomena as a pair of creamy cuffs, a bronzed skin, a collection of poems, a composed face.

8] And people *are* fooled by each other. They talk about each other, and to each other, in the most absurd circularities to keep the awkwardness of subjectivity out of their minds. 'Of course he's done well,' they say; 'he's got talent, he's got drive'. Or, 'It's easy for you to give up smoking – you've got willpower.' Or, 'It's one thing for a saint to endure suffering, it's another thing altogether for an ordinary person.'

People do what they do (we are almost crass enough to say) because they have a capacity to do so. They are what they are because it's their nature. And the clear evidence for the existence of this capacity and this nature is that they do what they do and are what they are.

[139] One is even persuaded to see certain aspects of one's own self in the same way. It's a relief to have one's failures explained as some kind of structural fault, about which one can do no more than can a piece of iron about its inherent weakness for combining with oxygen. Struggling to write, I seize hopefully on the notion that, having spent so much of my life writing, I have a talent for it – some kind of objective power inside myself, some sort of inner hardware, which will carry me through what seems as raw and clumsy a fight with words and the shifting world as any schoolchild ever fought in a post-Christmas thank you letter.

[140] – But some people can draw, and some people can't.
    – Some people do draw, and some people don't.
    – Some can but don't. Some would but can't.
    – In the case of drawing, I must admit, I see the incapacity sitting inside me as objective as a growth.

[141] 'The individual tends always to act so as to maximize his satisfaction.'
    With some formula like that, surely, we can get ourselves fixed into the objective universe, dissolve ourselves out. We've got *you* there, certainly, with your rather pretentious tastes in early keyboard music.

You're alongside all those people who sit half-asleep in front of their television sets every evening, too bored to get up and turn them off, and a lot of other people who maximize their satisfaction by having themselves tied up and whipped – which cuts you down to size a bit, I think. We've got all those people who maximized their satisfaction by preferring torture or death to betrayal. They're surprised to find themselves next to all the other people who maximized *their* satisfaction by preferring betrayal to torture or death. And there we all are, as helpless as inert masses in the grip of gravity.

And all of us colour-blind. Once again we have expanded into meaninglessness.

42] These psychologistic bubbles pop as soon as we touch them, like the theological bubbles of an earlier age. But they leave a faint odour of scepticism in the air, as the sonorous God-talk did of piety. We don't think quite the same with that smell in our nostrils. We don't feel as respectful as we did about the motives behind any behaviour. The feeling lingers that it's all some sort of self-gratification, one way or another; that each one of us is shut up inside himself, acting merely in order to produce an effect upon his own state of mind.

And sometimes we do behave like this. We know this kind of masturbatory feeling. But we recognize it by contrast with our feelings at other times! We don't start love-affairs to secure the stimulation of our pubic nerve. (That would be an insanely long way round to g about it, like buying a car to get the use of the cigar-lighter). We don't build sand-castles on the beach because it will induce a sense of achievement. The attraction is entirely different. The sand and water seem to offer certain possibilities which we could realize. Isn't it this sense of possibilities in the world around us which draws us on most of the time? Our objectives are external to us (even our unworthy ones). We want to see what can be shaped out of this material We want to outstrip our competitors. We want to see how our victim will behave when we hurt him. We want to assemble a solid, unbroken million pounds. We act upon the world, and the world acts upon us – and this involvement is characteristic of us.

[143] What we seek in a love-affair is not self-gratification; not even confirmation of our own objective reality, as in a mirror (though that comes into it); but an escape from the uniqueness of our own subjectivity. We want to come face to face with the naked subjectivity of another human being, and to feel that this other human being has come close to our own subjectivity. This is why the sexual act is feared. This is why we feel uneasy about the idea of its being watched. To a greater or lesser extent it symbolizes the self-revelation and self-dissolution of love.

4] Small children clamour to be thrown up in the air and swung round, to be treated like bundles of washing. Or they keep going round in circles until they're too dizzy to walk straight, and then they laugh at their helplessness. (Laugh *helplessly* at their helplessness.) I laughed helplessly the first time I was too drunk to walk straight, in the army – laughed all the way from the pub in town to the camp in the country outside, held up by my patient friends. It seemed to me very sweet to be a thing, without power or responsibility.

People cast themselves away, like old boots – into intoxication, into addiction to intoxicants, into love, into religious and political irresponsibility. Enthusiasts for political simplicities, when they get together, usually display much the same kind of behaviour as members of a rugby club after their annual dinner, the same aggressive bonhomie amongst themselves, the same desire to smash things up, the same boozy sentimentality and boozy hatreds.

Perhaps, when suicides throw themselves off high buildings, their last seconds of life are filled not with terror at all, but with peace – even with helpless laughter.

5] It's usually held that people smash things up because they don't understand them. Perhaps sometimes they do it for the opposite reason, too: because they do understand them, and wish to obliterate the meaning,

to halt, as by intoxication, the mind's endless reading.
Like a man who cannot sleep, and who turns from sid
to side trying to snap the endlessly unreeling thread o
thought.

[146] Another fix, another bottle – at least the addict has no
problem about his aims in life.

[147] What the alcoholic is after, says Berne, is not the
drunkenness but the hangover, and the drama of guilt
and shame and betrayal that goes with it. Jonathan
Miller has an appalling humorous story about when he
was on the wards, and a man was brought in suffering
from severe burns in his anus. It was getting near Guy
Fawkes Day, explained the patient, and nothing much
was happening, so he'd thought, here goes, I'll make
some trouble for someone. And he'd bought a rocket,
stuffed it up his arse, and lit the blue touchpaper.
    We set events in motion (some insane, some merely
banal) in order to get ourselves caught up in them, in
order to find ourselves being bundled helplessly on to
stretchers, in order to find ourselves compelled (as it
were in spite of ourselves) to work late every night, or
to lead love-lives like the second act of a farce.

[148] Someone from an underground newspaper said on a
television programme that his public was 'a set of
people who . . . mess themselves up on drugs, who
possibly fall down in the street, and to all these

gentlemen here are thoroughly obnoxious.' This sounds reassuringly like the stories people tell about alcoholics. About Dylan Thomas being sick in his soup, and the old actor saying, 'Just show me the stage, and tell me which play it is.'

The messing-up effect. The falling-down-in-the-street demonstration. We need some dark saints in our mythology who devote their lives to it. But we all experiment with a little degradation at some point in our lives. A little drunken vomiting down our waistcoats. A little dossing-down on benches and not changing our clothes. A little sleeping around with the wrong partners. Some people bear forever the traces of these *louche* tastes, like duelling scars.

They are among the *rites de passage* of our society; our own complex, and not entirely ritualized, form of circumcision upon entry into manhood; our own form of slashing our skins and rubbing dirt into the wounds.

9] We need to set a lower limit to ourselves. Or, at any rate, to have experimented with some of the lower possibilities. As we have experimented with some of the higher, in the impossible idealisms and religiosities of our mid-teens.

So, in later life, we are never quite as good as we hoped; nor quite as bad, either.

0] The paradigm of all drama (and perhaps of all narrative, too) is the Punch and Judy show. And the

essential characteristic of the Punch and Judy show is
this: that the performer *hides his face behind a curtain.*

[151] All over the world, in the drama of entirely
unconnected cultures, the actors conceal themselves
when they appear. They wear masks. They paint their
faces. They wear fantastic costumes. They speak in
unnatural voices. They speak in verse. They
communicate only by singing, or by dancing. Men
play women, women men. Naturalism is not natural;
it's a sophisticated late development that arrived in the
theatre at about the same time as the motor-car
arrived on the streets.

   Masking and disguise are fundamental not only to the
technique of drama but to its substance. Characters in
plays mask themselves so that they cannot be
recognized. They disguise themselves in order to be
taken for someone else. They are confused with twins
and doubles. They exchange clothes. Even without
disguise they are taken to be, or have to pass
themselves off as being, other than they are. They are
required to be one thing for one person, and at the
same time another for another. In 'psychological' plays
and films they take on the persona of another, are
possessed by the spirits of the dead, of themselves
when young.

   With each new device of concealment our appetite for
reading is stirred again. We see, with a kind of shock of
recognition, the gestures of human life in the crude
jerkings of the wooden puppets. We read, with a new

piquancy, the femininity of Rosalind through her assumed masculinity.

2] And it goes deeper than this. The flow of life out through the fingertips of the concealed puppeteer into his dolls, and the reading of one character into another, offers us an apparent overthrow of the distinction between subjectivity and objectivity, between one subjectivity and another. Symbolically, at any rate, when Chandebise (in *Une Puce à l'Oreille*) is kicked for the drunkenness of Poche, his double, and Poche is blamed for Chandebise's unfaithfulness, the unbreachable barrier between I and not-I seems to crumble (in the case of other I's, at any rate). We laugh because we seem to stand on the brink of seeing the natural order (indeed, the logical order) entirely overthrown, as when kings are made fools of and puns short-circuit the world's compartments.

53] Novelists, too, keep their faces hidden behind the curtain. Though sometimes they seem more like ventriloquists. They let themselves be seen, and keep their lips rigid while they make their dummies speak. Like ventriloquists, they side with the audience, and with normal social conventions, against the outrages committed by their dummies.

54] Other writers contrive a more subtle concealment by appearing to speak out *in propria persona*. But how grotesque these *personae* usually are! Great figures like

Easter Island totems, with huge sufferings, huge sensibilities, huge phalluses, huge rebellions. When you meet these writers in the flesh, at a party, they turn out to have dandruff, and be worrying about the rates and their children's education.

[155] And then we come to writers who present themselves in their writing as the sort of people you meet at parties suffering from dandruff, and worrying about the rates and their children's education. Like naturalism in the theatre, this is a late sophistication. Naturalistic representation is in general not easier but harder to read than stylized representation. It may well say less. When our symbols *resemble* what they represent, we teeter on the brink of nullity, on the edge of the Duchamps tautology, the urinal labelled 'Urinal'. Only the act of selection, of framing, of labelling, differentiates what is represented from what represents it. The challenge to our reading instinct here is one of minimality.

[156] The respectable citizens of some town in Germany, it was discovered, according to the papers, had been taking part in regular orgies. As each guest arrived at the orgy he took off all his clothes and put on a mask. No doubt their main intention was to conceal their identities; but also, I imagine, not to be recognized as selves, as the authors of their actions. As soon as people mask their faces they have a potential advantage over those around them, as Batman realized, and as all

children do as soon as one of them appears in a mask. Michael Argyle discovered, in a series of experiments at Oxford, that interview subjects were most disconcerted when their interlocutor concealed everything but his eyes. (When the interlocutor concealed his eyes as well, his subjects' uneasiness vanished. They spoke more freely even than when they could see all of him – as freely as to a priest, or to the psychiatrist who sits behind the head of the couch, or to God. To conceal my subjectivity but to see yours – this is what gives me the advantage.) If I came to your party in a mask I'd tell you a thing or two. It wouldn't be rates or secondary education I'd talk about.

7] I can't help feeling sceptical about the Bible's claim that God made man in his own image. What? Two solemn little Jehovahs to gaze back at him with fathomless wisdom and benevolence? What would have been the fun in that? He could have achieved *that* simply by creating a couple of mirrors, or a closed-circuit television.

The pleasure in creating life isn't a narcissistic one at all. It comes from the experience of moving outside oneself, of extending oneself (as it seems) into a subjectivity different from one's own. The puppeteer makes Punch with a hunched back and a hooked nose. (*He* doesn't look like that!) The grotesque creature runs amok up there on the finger-ends of his right hand, and murders the doll on his left hand. (*He* doesn't go round beating people to death!) The real pleasure in writing a novel comes when the characters one has so laboriously put together seem to take on a life of their own, as the phrase goes, and seize control of their destinies. Some authors, I suspect, attribute extravagant violence to their characters in the hope of simulating a spontaneity which refuses to develop. They try to generate independence by force. They hang exotic acts upon them – murder, rape, multiple murder, multiple rape – as if a slave ordered to dress as a tyrant were any less a slave.

[158] The moments which move a parent most are the ones when his child first sings a strange song, first tells a story from some inaccessible part of his own imagination, first acts on his own initiative, first suffers at the hands of the world.

What a strange tickling pleasure it must have given God, after his great solitude in a universe where there were only angels, bowing and scraping like footmen, to have children running between his feet, trying to make deals with him, the little monkeys, and speculating about his existence and morals – up to all their little murderous and blasphemous tricks!

[159] It's not just one's children. Any person with whom one's closely involved carries a little of one's subjectivity about with him. It gives me a small pleasurable shock, walking near my home, to catch

sight of my car passing along the street, being driven from somewhere to somewhere else by my wife; or to see her across the room at a party, laughing at some unheard conversation. It *is* a bit like catching an unexpected glimpse of yourself in a mirror – in a double mirror, a mirror mirrored. There you are suddenly, turning away from yourself quite independently to smile into a world beyond.

50] Each man in his time plays many parts. And not just for long runs, as Shakespeare seems to suggest, but in repertory – one part on Monday night, another on Tuesday, and a third at the Wednesday matinee. In these roles we give objective expression to ourselves. With some of my friends I'm the one who says, 'Let's do this! Let's do that!' With others I play the cautious man who always sees the drawbacks to things, and wants to do the washing-up before having the coffee. Both these roles feel slightly false, but by alternating between them a kind of dialectic is maintained. I should feel uneasy if some sudden limitation of my circle of friends reduced me to playing only one of them. (There are other roles which I feel would destroy me if circumstances reduced me to playing them continuously.)

Why don't I *be myself*? I am being myself. These roles are both aspects of myself. I have more of myself to go round that I can distribute at one dinner party.

Then why am I inconsistent in the way I distribute

myself? Why do I distribute all the enthusiasm here, and all the scepticism there? For the same reason that the champagne manufacturers sell all the dry champagne in England and all the sweet in America: because that's where the markets are.

[161] Laing speaks as if we were dummies, on whom roles were hung like suits of clothes. But (by Laing's own account) we are actors, not dummies. We are not inert, even the most passive of us; the roles we play are not simply thrust upon us. They are arrived at, as it were, by consultation between us and the director. The management wishes us to play the ungrateful delinquent son (let's say). But we have our own careers to consider. We insist that certain lines are cut. We will not play the nude scene. We twist the part to bring out the vulnerability and charm of the character. With luck and skill we steal the play – and go on to other and bigger productions.

What I am is the product of a number of factors. One of these factors is myself.

Even if I try to submerge myself totally in the part, even if I follow slavishly every slightest requirement and suggestion of the management, I shall play the part differently from anybody else.

If we were all dummies, my suit of clothes would have been hung on me by a dummy, whose own suit of clothes would have been hung on him by a dummy . . . Somewhere a living hand must have been raised, scissors taken up, needles threaded.

62] Laing speaks as if to play a role were to become a
zombie, one of the walking dead. We don't think of
actors becoming zombies when they appear on the
stage. We envisage the deployment of a fairly high-
order skill, and of certain qualities of spirit such as
spontaneity and confidence and responsiveness. We
see an actor as enlarged by the parts he plays; as
expressing himself through them; as being released by
them from nullity and silence.

When you, politely reading this, enable me to be for a
time the Wise Father I *rejoice* in the part. I surpass
myself. Words come to me. Thoughts unfold.

Laing may take similar pleasure in the part which we
have between us set up for him.

63] Roles offer us forms of being.

Laing has a Presbyterian distrust of the theatre, that's
his trouble.

And aren't novelists playing the same game? And
poets? And painters? Structuring up little false fronts
with the intention of communicating? (Entering into a
psychodrama with the observer.)

64] We need an audience (a family, friends) before whom
we can *act out* our grief and our joy. We give our grief
expression by playing the part of the bereaved man.
We externalize it, get it out of ourselves, come to terms
with it – and are enabled to continue with our life.

[165]   What would we be like if we put all our roles off, and emerged from behind them? We smile and stretch, reborn, untrammelled: Now we are playing the role of one who has put his roles off.

[166]   We detect coherent roles in the confusion of other people's behaviour (and of our own) in order to make sense of it. We *must* have certain forms through which to see each other (and ourselves). We *must* have certain expectations of each other (and of ourselves). This is what it is to know people (and to know ourselves). If their personalities had no stable contours in our minds, they would be chaos, not persons.

[167]   Until we are known to others in this way, we feel ourselves undefined, undifferentiated from the background, unreal.

And as soon as we *are* known in this way, we feel ourselves slightly oppressed, slightly belittled. We don't want to be too closely characterized, too predictable. 'Just like you!' you say to me – and I feel a bit of a fool. I sulk away from it.

We all hold many surprises for each other. Some are frequently surprising that we cling to this very characteristic as a stable trait. We expect them to do what we don't expect. 'Just like you!' we cry, as once again they do something which is unlike them. One can easily imagine them feeling oppressed and belittled by *this*. They would like to escape into predictability for once.

8] Our perception of the world in general is rather like our perception of people. We assign roles even to inanimate objects. Or rather, we cast them according to the possibilities they seem to offer, and direct them to bring those possibilities out.

9] In some philosophical moods perception appears as a state of passive receptivity. The world is full of distinguishable objects (it seems) whose nature, shape and definition are part of themselves. We open our eyes; the objects before us imprint themselves on our retinas; we attach a name to each object and thereby make it accessible to the operations of language.

In other philosophical moods it appears that our perception is the active element in the universe. The world is full of chaos. By an act of perception we place constructions upon it. Until we *see* trees – pick out one lot of shapes from all the others, and conceptualize a class of trees by deciding to see all these shapes (each one of them different, after all) *as* trees, and all those *not* as trees – trees don't exist.

But isn't it, to put it in a weird way, more like a dialogue? The phenomena before us have their possibilities. We seize upon these possibilities, this way or that way, depending upon our needs and interests. Our needs interlock with certain possibilities.

I need twenty dancers for the show, and find them. But each of them has other possibilities. Anne also sings: she might have found herself, if she'd gone to another audition for a different producer, in a chorus.

Diane is a trained nurse: she might have found herself as one of the nurses at a certain hospital. Cheryl is a depressive: one more day out of work and she might have been one of the patients in the ward where Diane was a nurse.

But to me, as I sit there in the empty stalls, chewing my cigar, they're dancers. Not singers, nurses and depressives who can also dance. Just dancers.

[170]   I look out of the window, testing this view. Six elm trees rise from mown grass. Cars flash by along the roads. The whole scene looks very cut and dried. What other possibilities could those elm trees have but to be elm trees? How could I redirect the scene in my mind so that I couldn't see a difference between the trees and the grass, or the trees and the cars?

But looking at the view out of my window isn't a piece of primitive perception. Most of the perception's been done already. The view out of my window (and out of yours, I think) has already been given shape and form by the efforts of men to modify the world to fit their own categorizations. The cars and roads have been built to fulfil their defining functions (mechanical dancers, without larynxes or emotions). The trees have been separated out from the confusion of the primeval forest, first by the hunters who categorized them in order to be able to find their way, then by the naturalists and gardeners and landscape architects who transplanted them into unambiguous situations.

Now think of the world covered with primeval forest. Suddenly it seems a bit less cut and dried. Though in fact we are coming back to it with an immense equipment of conceptualization already assembled. We've seen pictures and specimens of most of the types of vegetation. We're clear (fairly clear) about branches and leaves and snakes . . .

Now think of looking through a microscope at some world of organisms you've never seen before. Baffled, you sort out the confusion with concepts brought from the macroscopic world. There are some things that look like threads of cotton . . . some groups of dots . . . some things with branches, like trees . . . The biologist with you smiles. You haven't seen the characteristic stippling of the background tone, of which this is (for him) a specimen. (The 'threads' are in fact the same as the 'trees'. The dots are irrelevant intrusions.)

71] You look again. Y-e-e-e-s. You *think* you see what he means.
        – Have a look at this slide, then.
        – There it is again! The same thing exactly!
        – No, this is something else altogether.

72] But those 'threads', those 'trees', you certainly saw *them*, even if not in the same way that a biologist does. You saw them because they presented themselves to you as 'threads' and 'trees'. The primeval forest, if you'd never seen a tree, might have presented itself to

you as 'arms' and 'legs'. You wouldn't have been
fooled. You wouldn't have thought it was people. But
you might have been enabled to see it as a kind of
extension and distortion of the world of arms and legs,
while knowing they were not – just as you did not for
one moment suppose that the 'threads' and 'trees' were
in any sense threads or trees.

What we see, we see from the very first *as* something.
This is how we enable it to present itself to us. What
we cannot see *as* something, we do not see at all.

[173] This process of analogy has to start somewhere. A
child must learn to see a first thing without the help of
it. So must a man who gains his sight after congenital
blindness. (Human beings are complex; the world is
complex; there are ways round everything.) But it's
evidently a slow and difficult step. And after it's been
made our experience does not consist of taking in (as it
were) neutral visual material, and constructing bits of
the world out of it. We see *things*, even if we see them
with conscious reservations about the analogies we have
used (as with the 'threads'), even if we know that we
shall come to see them differently.

This isn't the case with our other senses. The sound
tastes, smells, and tactile sensations which we
experience are not given form in this way. They come
to us detached from the world of objects, without
ontological status. Sounds and smells are 'given off',
and then wander about freely in their own right;

flavours can be lost, like labels. Tactile sensations are different again: we feel a *something*, not an emanation of a something, but we don't necessarily feel the something *as* a this or a that. When it's beneath our fingertips in the darkness, say, or pressing into our back, we may work out a hypothesis quite slowly and consciously, or not even attempt one.

I hear the sound of a car. I smell a strange smell. I taste a flavour like nothing I've ever tasted before. I feel an unexplained pressure against my knee. There's nothing odd or 'philosophical' about these usages.

But: I see the sight of a car. I see a strange appearance. I experience an unexplained visual emanation. These, if anything, are translations made in the light of some highly suspect philosophical theory.

4] You look out of the window, and something, in the twilight, catches the corner of your eye, and is gone again before you can turn.

'I saw something . . .' you say. I ask what it was like.

'I don't know. Something . . . strange . . . I can't describe it.'

But you can say something about it. Something about the space that surrounded it: 'The leaves moved.' 'For a moment it looked almost like a face.' Or you could extend one of our indefinite categories to find some kind of match for it: 'It was a kind of grey blur across the path.'

A minimal case of seeing. But still it's a question of

seeing *something*. Still there's no question of experiencing some kind of raw visual data. In so far as any seeing has been done here, it's because you've been able to place some construction on the event, however vague.

[175] Michel Tournier, in *Friday*, his rewriting of the Robinson Crusoe story, opposes the 'Western' relationship of Robinson to his surroundings (cultivation, organization, the establishment of laws and institutions, labour and domination) and the 'solar' relationship which he later learns from Man Friday (harmonious co-existence, wordless acceptance, joyous immersion). As if those who lived by hunting and gathering (like Friday) did not also perceive their surroundings by organizing and structuring them, and survive by dominating their environment in their own fashion. We sit over our coffee and yearn to be just a species among species, to live with the wordless simplicity of animals. (And yet to know that we are so living!) But even the tiger has structured his perception of the world to yield the shape of the gazelle; and the gazelle the tiger. Where must we look to find the wordless communion with the universe which haunts our imagination? In *Friday*, by Michel Tournier; in stories; in words.

[176] In perception, I'd like to say, we elucidate the bits of the world before us by holding up against them the bi

of the world we already know. (And, in so doing, increase the stock of known bits for the future.) Such a process can be undertaken because the possibilities of order exist (stability, differentiability).

7] The development of the child towards understanding: the acquisition of a context in which its experiences have meaning.

8] Hold up your hand in front of you. Now give me a complete description of it.

And you can't. Nothing that you can ever say will wholly describe the one thing that now lies in front of your eyes. You could describe away until the crack of doom. You could describe it as a whole, millimetre by millimetre, cell by cell, molecule by molecule. You could pile statement upon statement, and just as many more statements would remain to be made. And I should still not have available to me as much information as your first casual glance made available to you.

9] Look at your hand. The central assumption of Western philosophy (of all Western thinking, one might say) crumbles before your eyes.

I mean the assumption, implicit or explicit, that the world is a complex of definite states of affairs (of qualities, of relationships) which can, at any rate in theory, be given definite expression in definite assertions. I mean the assumption which underlies the syllogism, and Leibniz's conception of a subject-predicate universe; the assumption which was systematized in the picture given by logical atomism of a world consisting of facts which are mirrored in the propositions of language.

Of course, philosophers have turned the page from this picture. They now insist on the multifariousness of language, and show to how many other uses it can be put apart from making factual statements. But they talk as if the problem is to sort out the factual from the non-factual uses. They don't seem to doubt that there are some sorts of statement which have a kind of concrete relationship with concrete aspects of the universe, that everything in the universe has its parallel in language, a slot waiting for it.

And not only philosophers talk like this. Novelists labour to avoid 'interpretation' by listing events and bald descriptions. People (intelligent people) ask patiently why newspapers don't 'confine themselves to the facts'.

[180]   Look at your hand. Its structure does not match the structure of assertions, the structure of facts. Your hand is continuous. Assertions and facts are discontinuous.

Look at the gradients of the surface. Look at the graduation of the colour. You lift your index finger half an inch; it passes through a million facts.

Look at the way your hand goes on and on, while the clock ticks, and the sun moves a little further across the sky.

Think of the distance between your hand and your eye, between your hand and Alpha Centauri, between your hand and the bottom right hinge on the West Door of York Minster.

81]   Of course, you can tell me the distance between your hand and Alpha Centauri. You can take up any particular point that I wish, or that you wish. You can isolate any aspect you choose, and draw my attention to it.

You can mark two points on a sheet of paper and draw a line between them. There are an infinite number of places where you can mark the points, and an infinite number of different lines that would connect them.

Could you in theory mark all the points, and draw all the lines?

Would you feel that the nature of the paper had been more thoroughly explored if you could, and did, and its surface were covered with an even sheen of graphite?

Do you need to feel that there exists, on the surface of the virgin sheet of paper, an infinite number of potential points and lines?

To mark a point, to draw a line, is to *distinguish* it, to *nominate* it.

82]   But *really* (you object) the facts are all there, waiting to be given expression in statements.

Then *really* we are all colour-blind, and this aspect of

the world is waiting only to be given expression in stricter standards.

[183] I ask you about the width of your hand, or you volunteer information about its colour, in order to separate these aspects out from all the others. I can imagine circumstances where we'd want a general description of your hand: to distinguish it from other hands (because a witness saw one of the murderer's hands, let's say), or because your hand is to be used as a sample of one sort of hands (white, female, class A/B Rhesus positive) for my definitive study 'Hands, Classified by Race, Sex, Class and Blood Group'. Facts don't lie about like pebbles on the beach. They relate to particular purposes, particular contexts.

[184] The purposes needn't be practical. I can imagine your writing a description of your hand in your autobiography, as a kind of capricious aside. 'My hand rests on the paper in front of me as I write, the skin grained like an old tobacco-pouch, the tendons moving beneath the surface like passing thoughts.' But I feel you have a literary purpose in mind. You're suggesting a certain view of yourself – perhaps a certain view of the way you see yourself.

Or I can imagine your offering the description even more waywardly, without any literary intent. Suddenly during a pause in the conversation, à propos of nothing, you look at your hand and say dreamily: 'The skin's grained like an old tobacco-pouch. The tendons move under the surface like passing moles.' We're sitting in some café on holiday, say, waiting for the rain to stop. And probably I go on looking out of the window, watching the people hurry by with newspapers over their heads, not paying much attention. A minimal situation. But even here, something struck you to make you speak – one aspect out of all the aspects made you exclaim.

35] In philosophical writing you sometimes get the feeling that the complete situation is this: the world is given expression in language. This is a bit like seeing air travel as people getting on to planes. We're only looking at half the situation – they also get off at the other end. And this is the *point* of air travel – not that you get from London to an air liner, or from an air liner to New York, but that you get from London to New York.

Your description of your hand has not reached its destination in your uttering of the words. It reaches its destination when I understand the words.

Language is not the world talking about itself.

Language is you talking to me about the world.

Language is as between you and me.

6] Or between you and yourself. You, too, understand what you say. You, by your choice of words, isolate and identify aspects of the world for yourself, as well.

When you say that the skin of your hand is grained like a tobacco-pouch, you use the language notation to bring into juxtaposition, both for yourself and for me, two different parts of the world (your hand, a tobacco-pouch). We are dealing in bits of the world.

[187] You tell me that your hand is brown, is 8.4 centimetres wide at its widest. Are we dealing in 'bits' of the world here? Aren't we talking about one bit and its internal qualities, its internal relationships?
– We're bringing your hand into juxtaposition with the other brown things of our experience, dead leaves, wood and tobacco-pouches; and with the section of a ruler marked off by the 8.4 centimetre mark, and other objects in the world of the same length.
   You want to protest that this is a circularity, that what these things have in common is precisely the fact that they are brown, or 8.4 centimetres long. But couldn't I, instead of speaking, silently hold first a dead leaf against your hand, and then a piece of wood, and then a tobacco-pouch, and so on, until you see the likeness?
– Then there *is* a likeness! Likeness inheres in them!
– To *my* eye, Polonius, yonder cloud is like a weasel. Is its weasel-likeness inherent in it? Internal to it? Is the fact that this cloud is weasel-like a part of the universe? Is the fact that this cloud is weasel-like to my eye but to no one else's part of the universe?

[188] The world doesn't get itself lodged in language as in a museum, and left there for anyone to come and

inspect. 'My hand is 8.4 centimetres wide' has no meaning at all outside some particular situation, some particular context. Nor does even the most general-sounding statement ('Man is a featherless biped'). If this is not immediately obvious to us, it's because we begin, as soon as we hear the words, to imagine possible contexts for them.

89] Written up in the middle of some expanse of concrete beside an urban motorway: 'God is Alive and Well and Living in Denver.' You don't know who wrote it, or who specifically it's intended for, and it's surrounded by nothing but concrete. All the same, it's *thick* with context.

A single sentence comes to light on a tablet in some new excavation. 'Epimenides the Cretan paid four measures of oil and three of corn.' At once we begin to visualize the situation in which this statement might have played its part.

90] What philosophers have often claimed to be concerned with is truth. But has any philosopher ever managed to say very much that wasn't later meticulously denied by other philosophers? While you and I, going about our ordinary business, manage to speak the truth almost all the time! Or at any rate to say things which are not on the whole systematically denied by our friends and colleagues.

91] The truth is that the question of truth does not occur all that often in ordinary life. We raise it normally only to distinguish cases of deliberate deception and wilful misrepresentation, or in selecting one account from conflicting variants. We are even chary of calling error falsehood, and its correction truth. When philosophers tell us that there is some *general* difficulty about establishing the truth – that our senses may deceive us, that we live in a world of mere appearances, that the forms of language may conceal the real structure of the world – they are extending this technique of distinction to the point where the distinction is obliterated. They are telling us that the whole population may be colour-blind.

[192] The whole of logic turns upon this distinction between true and false. It asserts that if there are any propositions in the world, then some of them are true and some of them are false. For one of the fundamental formulations of the propositional calculus is this: that 'Either P or not-P' is true for all values of P. That is to say, that every proposition has its negative counterpart; that out of each pair one must be true and one must be false; and that for each of these pairs a further (second-order) proposition is true – namely, that one proposition in the original pair is true and the other false.

True/false; on/off; yes/no. For a proposition to be simply true, when the only alternative is for it to be simply false, there must exist in the world some isolable state of affairs which it could wholly embody, or to which it could wholly correspond.

93] We've been speaking the truth all day since we got up, but to how many of the things we've said should we consider attaching this simple, unqualified seal? We feel it wasn't like that at all. Do we mean that the things we said were *possible* (this is the kind of alternative truth-value that philosophers have suggested)? Or that they could have been analysed into elements which would be simply true, or simply false? It wasn't like that either! We said this kind of thing: 'The car keys are by the front door,' 'You're looking a bit seedy this morning,' 'A fool and his money are soon parted.' How near to a front door do car keys have to be for my statement to be simply true, and how far away for it to be simply false? And I don't mean it's *possible* that they're by the front door! They *are* by the front door – I'm looking at them now! And what I mean couldn't be analysed into statements about keys (or appearances of keys) being 29.731 centimetres from a door (or an appearance of a door), because I don't know exactly how far it is, and don't care. I feel like saying, in this case, that what I said was reasonable, useful, helpful. Does 'A and (If A then B)' entail B, as logic maintains, when what I am claiming in giving A is not that it is true, but that it is a helpful thing to say?

4] But supposing I measure the distance between the front door and the car keys, and it comes to 29.731 centimetres. Now surely the statement that the car keys are 29.731 centimetres from the front door is quite simply true, does quite simply and wholly express a particular and isolable state of affairs?

It has this air because to some extent the sentence is merely a translation out of one notation into another. There is a simple translational relationship between that particular mark on the ruler and its verbal expression.

But when we go back to the circumstances which the original act of notation expressed, all the usual idiotic indefiniteness reappears. 29.731 centimetres between which key and which part of the front door? Childish quibbles! (But they might not be, in certain circumstances.) We nominate points. But won't our nomenclature always leave some slight (perhaps sub-microscopic) play?

[195] 'Napoleon was defeated at Waterloo.'
'Igniting hydrogen in an atmosphere of oxygen produces water.'
'Dairy products are among the principal exports of New Zealand.'
Aren't these statements simply and wholly true? Couldn't they be fed into the propositional calculus with the utmost confidence?

Statements like these have an air of such simple and uncomplicated truth because they are rehearsals of what we have already accepted into the corpus of our knowledge. When we say them now they ring out confidently – not because they chime with events, but because they chime with earlier statements which we have already accepted as true. When do we say 'Napoleon was defeated at Waterloo'? When we produce our stock of knowledge in examinations. When we transmit our traditions to our children. When we remind each other in discussion of certain fixed points that we all accept.

But it was very different for the journalist who sent the original story, trying to condense the events of those three days into a single sentence. Is 'Waterloo' right? Mightn't it equally well be Quatre-Bras or Ligny? And to talk about *Napoleon* – isn't that personalized journalism of a rather suspect type, a crude shorthand for something much more complicated? And mightn't 'defeated' be a bit strong?

When we say, now, that 'Napoleon was defeated at Waterloo' is true, it's not because we check that statement against the events, even in our mind, but because we check the statement against other statements. A weird parallel appears with logical necessity. Things seem simple because we are working in an enclosed world of symbols, whose reference has been excluded from our current operations.

6] You might say of the attempts you are now making to describe your current original observations that they will ripen into this closed system of falsehood/truth with age, as a congenial system of statements accrues around them, or fails to.

[197] But in the first place our statements of fact are based upon evidence. And what counts as evidence? Documents, statements by witnesses, photographs, the readings on scientific instruments – constructs already in various notations.

[198] But the evidence which the witnesses give in their statements is based upon the evidence of their senses.
   'The evidence of their senses'! As if their senses spoke! As if their eyes had, in some internal court, taken the oath and testified!

[199] We get inside our notations, and draw the cutains and refuse to look out; and everything seems comparativel simple.

[200] Of course, we know how to operate a simple binary system with the values true/false. But when we call a statement about the world true in this simple on/off way, it's not that we recognize in it some absolute incarnation of a particular state of affairs, but that we *commit* ourselves to it. It's a little like committing ourselves to a policy, or a course of action. We don't for a moment imagine that any one policy is likely to meet the case entirely, but something has to be done – either we must take *this* path or we must take *that* path. So, in certain circumstances, something has to be said, either that the goal *was* scored or that it *wasn't*.

1] If, indeed, we ever make anything that might be described as a statement about the world. Isn't there an element of *pronouncement* in almost everything we say? (Of delivering judgment.) Or of naming? Or of exclaiming? Or of persuading? We don't go through life announcing neutrally what is the case. We're not speaking clocks!

2] In a sudden flash you see the deep and immutable truth about how things stand, and cry out with it. And at once you feel that you might well have said exactly the opposite with no less justice, and no less sense of illumination.

3] So you failed to say it. Never mind. All the more reason for trying again.

4] And I may find the ninety-nine times you get it wrong more stimulating to my imagination than the one time you come near to getting it right. If there *were* such a thing as a statement, and if a statement could be entirely correct and complete, there would be nothing to say in reply to it except 'yes'. Who wants to take part in a conversation where 'yes' is the only contribution you can make?

5] There's something too neat, too cut and dried, about all our formulations. People talk about 'moral choice'.

The phrase suggests the closed-ended intelligence test, with four possible answers provided, only one of them correct. And of course we are sometimes presented with clear-cut choices like this. But to generalize from these instances, to make them the archetype, is to be carried away by a literary convention, a device which writers use in order to simplify and dramatize. Our moral behaviour in general is as open-ended as everything else. We don't choose a moral response, we construct one. We see what we can make out of the materials that come to hand. And its 'rightness' or 'wrongness' rarely become unambiguously clear, any more than the rightness or wrongness of a house, or of an economic plan.

Even to speak of 'a moral response' is too neat. We construct responses to the world (and make our own *démarches*, to which the world in its turn responds). The responses are practical. They have a moral aspect in the way that they may have an aesthetic or a political aspect.

And for all these aspects, a context is needed. A man hands money to another; drives steel into flesh; travels from Rome to Oslo. One can imagine contexts in which all these acts have moral (and political) significance. Without a context they don't even have a practical significance.

[206]   The central tradition of literature is not description or historical narrative but storytelling; the creation of a

fictitious world. Even where the old stories were about actual events and personages they were embodied in fictions, in parallels with the real world rather than representations of it. The factual possibilities of literature are a late departure. Looking at (say) the Old Testament, you might come to feel that fiction isn't an extension of fact, but that fact is a special case of fiction.

7]   The great pleasure of fiction is that it *is* fiction – another world, set among the world we know, often overlapping with it, often aping it, but essentially not it. We read ourselves and our world in it. Its evocativeness consists in this: that we detect a sense of familiarity in its strangeness. Just as a familiar smell in unfamiliar surroundings can suddenly evoke with great intensity a whole world we took for granted when it was before our eyes.

8]   The impossibility of sagas, of heroic history, is the sign of their otherness. If there could be such a thing as pure history it would be the limiting case of the story, where all otherness had been removed. The pure history of the Hundred Years War would be the Hundred Years War.

9]   One of the piquancies of art is how much like a part of the natural world it can make itself, while still being not a part of the natural world. And then, when we start to take that for granted, artists devise another relish: they show us how *unlike* the natural world a representation can be, and yet still enable us to read some aspect of the natural world within it.

[210] ˙ We hesitate to call photography an art because we feel that here the first process has moved to the brink of tautology. A photograph is not something fashioned to look like the natural world; it *is* the natural world, refracted through a lens. The otherness has dissolved in our hands. We feel most inclined to call photograph works of art when we are most clearly reminded of the difference to our perception of this natural world that the interposition of a lens and a shutter and a light-sensitive surface can make. These are signs of photography's otherness: instantaneousness, motionlessness, monochromatism, rectangularity, differential focus; the revelation of (for instance) momentary shadows of weariness and despair passing across usually composed faces, and of the static positions comprised in rapid motion. Each technical advance – motion, colour, sound, wide vision, deep focus – has begun by making photographs not more compelling but more insipid. The insipidity has been overcome only as photographers have learnt to introduce new signs of otherness, new artificialities, to compensate: speeded-up and slowed-down motion, stop-shots, deliberate distortions of colour values, grain, unnatural lighting effects, contrary framing, blurred movement, halation.

1] One of the signs of otherness that photography offers is a change of scale: the hugeness of close-ups in the cinema, the graspable smallness of snapshots. This is the piquancy of toys and scale models – and of those distant views, from hills and from the air, which seem to reduce whole cities and whole landscapes to scale models of themselves.

2] Art celebrates, mourns, mocks . . . and *names*. It creates handles by which we seize hold of the world. (The pleasure of turning a piece of sculpture over in your hands.) So do natural laws, and elementary particles. Once again we are holding up different bits of the world against each other – stone against flesh, legislation against causality, electricity against matter.

3] Scientists sometimes talk as if the point of their discoveries were the revelation of the world's structure. But the point of propounding a structure is to elucidate what lies before our eyes. The point of all explanation is that the general should illuminate the particular, not the particular the general.

4] What keeps our attention in stories is wanting to know what happens next. Odd, then, that almost all novels have been written in the past tense. (The occasional use of the present, one can't help feeling, is a dramatic extension, a device which gains most of its force from the contrast with the main tradition.) What intrigues us is not the uncertainty of what will happen next, as in life, but, on the contrary, the certainty of it. The girl goes to her lover's flat, summoned by an urgent telephone message. But she arrives to find the flat apparently empty, goes in, and – as the chapter ends – hears the front door being quietly locked behind her. We don't know what's happening, but we know that the author does. It's all been decided. The girl has been brought to the flat because certain events are to happen. The cadence of the whole story is already prepared and secure – already there, already recorded on pages we are actually holding in our hands. All we have to do is to continue to read. The world of the novel (and of the history book) is enclosed. What was and is and will be is all there, between a front cover and a back. It's not open to the incomprehensibility of the real present, and the uncertainty of the real future.

[215] And it's independent of us. It requires no effort or decision from us.

In the theatre sometimes attempts are made to break out of this enclosure. Characters – or the actors playing them – address the audience directly, speak to them individually, invite their participation. But all these tricks serve only to emphasize the real logic of the situation. The archetype of all this is in the pantomime, when Jack asks the children to shout out and warn him if the robbers appear. But the comedy is that when the children do shout, Jack doesn't hear them, or doesn't look round in time, or looks in the wrong direction. This is what drives the audience to hysteria – their inability to influence the action even when they try.

The essence of the story is that the audience *doesn't* participate. Things roll forward ineluctably. We watch aghast, or comically anguished. We see a world from which we are absent, a world in which the Indeterminacy Principle has been suspended, so that we are able to observe without our presence altering what we observe.

6] Considering language 'philosophically', one forgets how heavily it depends upon metaphor. Even the most unimaginative and literal-minded people think of themselves as being filled with despair, heartbroken, consumed with curiosity, swayed by arguments, and eaten with remorse. Indeed, there's almost nothing one can say about one's mental and emotional experience without speaking entirely in metaphor. 'Gloom', 'depression', 'frame of mind' – these are all metaphors. So, in a way, are terms like 'feeling' and 'sensation', when used in expressions such as 'feelings of happiness' and 'sensations of relief': they express mental states in terms of what goes on at the nerve-ends. You shift back into ever more scientific-sounding language – 'reactions', 'affective tones'. Now we are using the physical sciences to provide metaphors. We're drawing analogies between the

behaviour of human beings and the behaviour of
billiard balls, between mental states and colour.

Even in the physical world we rely heavily upon the
crossovers of metaphor. To describe sound, for
instance, we cast about all over the place. Think of the
provenance of 'tone', 'sharp', 'flat', 'sweet', 'hot',
'glissando'.

Not that we do think of the provenance. One of the
general movements of language is from the
metaphorical to the concrete. The metaphoricality of
expressions evaporates over the years. We don't, each
time we describe someone as depressed, go back to
some kind of image of physical lowering. But
something lingers, some kind of association with
lowering. When we're depressed, when we feel low,
we do physically . . . sort of . . . *feel low*.

[217] Yes, when we're torn with indecision we can almost
feel the one half parting company from the other half.
When we're sunk in despondency we can almost feel
ourselves resting at a hopeless angle on the sea-bottom,
half-full of sand, our iron cannon scattered among the
coral.

And yet, when you stand back and think about them,
how arbitrary our usage of metaphors like this comes
to seem! We cram the shifting flux of our feelings into
these familiar containers almost at random. You can
imagine someone crying out, 'I'm filled with despair!'
And this seems perfectly definite, entirely concrete.
But then someone else, anxious to get things right,

asks, 'Are you sure that it's not that you're rent by remorse?' And you can imagine that after a moment's thought the first man might slap his forehead in amazement. 'Yes!' he shouts. 'It's remorse, not despair! And I'm rent, not filled!'

8] This has nothing to do with the banality of these homely metaphors. The more subtly and precisely writers try to describe their characters' thoughts and feelings, the more constructed and arbitrary their representations have to be. With the microscopic examination of motive and feeling in writers like James and Musil one feels that one is entering a world of symbolization as abstract and self-contained as a ballet. In matters of this sort, precision is the most artificial convention of all.

9] In fact, the more one thinks about our common kit of metaphors for mental states and events, the less inclined one is to take it for granted, or dismiss it as banal. 'At the back of one's mind', 'to run over the alternatives', 'to reach a decision', 'something stirred in her memory', 'he groped for words' – they're brilliant! A whole literature, really, trodden down into the soil like last year's leaves, fertilizing, unrecognized and forgotten, whatever pushes above the ground now.

20] Among the complex of sensations and states which press in upon us and pass over us are moments of elation and dejection. To give them describable shape and substance we see them as intimations, as glimpses of more solid and continuing states. We pick out among the transient feelings the regular pattern of happiness, say, or of sadness. Language (and art, and mythology) is an attempt to body forth these states, to fill in the continuing texture of them between glimpses. We tell ourselves stories of happiness (of love, of piety) to give ourselves a context in which to place these shifting lights and tones.

[221] Even mathematics is a metaphor.
It's the metaphor of the hand: a way of seeing the world in terms of one's fingers. To take a mental hold on the multiplicity of the world, I say, 'It's as if I stretched out the fingers of my left hand, and then *these* fingers on my right hand as well.' Or, 'It's as if I stretched out all my fingers, and then did it again alongside, and then again and again . . .' Or, 'It's as if this one single object were divided (as my hand is), and this bit corresponded to my little finger, this to my fourth finger . . .'

[222] The whole of arithmetic is really this one concrete metaphor of the human hand. All operations with numbers are in essence counting, and short cuts to save counting all over again: that's to say, bringing the world into comparison with our fingers.

[223] You look uneasy. You think we've fallen into circularity. What the seven days of the week have in

common with the seven fingers I'm holding up, you want to say, is the very fact that there are seven of each!

What the seven days of the week have in common with each other is the fact that they're days of the week.

What this cloud has in common with a weasel is the fact that (to me) they look similar.

Is there some dayishness over and above the seven days of the week? Something that exists independently of them?

Is there, in the cloud and in the weasel, some quality of looking (to me) similar?

24] You're confused by the complicatedness of seven. Think of binary mathematics, where everything is expressed in terms of two symbols only. Does the one have in common with this one book *the fact that* there is one of each? Does the zero have in common with the absence of books on the floor *the fact that* there is none of either?

Binary mathematics needn't even be expressed in digits. The two possibilities of an electric circuit, on and off, say just as much. Do you really want to say that the existence of an electrical potential in this circuit has some *fact* in common with this book?

25] Binary mathematics, and bi-valued logic, is the metaphor of day and night. Or, if you prefer, of waking and sleeping. Or sun and rain. Or in and out. But of *something*! Or of a number of things. We are seeing the world in terms of itself.

[226]   Logic takes a hold on the subtle gradations and
         unevennesses and compromises of the world by
         saying it's as if it were either day or night, either
         white or black, either true or false. Its metaphoricality,
         its as-if nature, becomes clear when you examine how
         conventional the true/false dichotomy is in practice.
         It's not in the nature of language to seize the world so
         unambiguously! (Or of the world to be so seized.) But
         then, is night ever absolutely dark, or day absolutely
         bright?

[227]   You think of mathematics as something abstract,
         something entire unto itself, over and above the gross
         particularity of the world, something that would still
         be true even if nothing existed. Of empty universes
         one can say either nothing or everything. If it would
         still be true that $2+3=5$ in a world where there were
         no five things, then it would still be true that
         $2H+O=H_2O$ in a world which didn't in fact happen
         to contain either hydrogen or oxygen.

[228]   You're worried by the knowledge that logicians have
         demonstrated mathematics to be derived from a
         handful of occult axioms. But then you're worried,
         too, about the 'deep grammar' which underlies
         language, according to modern linguistics. You think
         that in the depths of our notations something
         profound lies hidden.

9] Where among our fingers is the square root of minus one? Where is our first transfinite finger?

One might equally well object: where is the celebrated Golden Mountain? Where is the notorious present King of France? And indeed, which of all the women in the world is Cinderella? Which of all the eggs Humpty Dumpty?

Our notation of words and numbers enables us to set up fictitious (and indeed impossible) reflections and distortions of the world. So do mirrors and lenses, and other instruments. Our number notation enables us to produce ghost images of fingers, and mirror-images of fingers that recede into glass-green infinity.

0] What makes the world susceptible to mathematics is our act of quantification; our decision as to what in any particular case will constitute a unit. What makes the world susceptible to logic is our act of classification; our decision as to what in any particular case will come under which heading. And *these* acts are not deductive. They are judgments – acts of discovery and commitment – with their analogies in art.

1] – But the world *is* mathematical! The spiral of the snail shell follows the intervals of the Fibonacci series . . .
– There are regularities in the universe. We find that to identify and describe them we can say, 'Look, it's *as if*

at the first turn of the spiral I held out one finger, at the second another finger, at the third another two fingers . . .'

[232] If the world were not full of regularities and repetitions – if we were, for example, disembodied consciousnesses floating in a sea of cloud – we shouldn't have either a mathematics or a language. (And most of the more accessible regularities and repetitions arise from the reproductive nature of the biological process, and from the purposive nature of our own activity. Trees are like trees because they are reproductions of trees. Chairs are like chairs because they are all for sitting on.)

[233] Is there an order in the universe?
– There are orders. And disorders.

[234] We marvel at the mathematicality of the snail shell. But we marvel at it for its contrast with the random geometry of the ground over which the snail creeps, and the random arrangement of the heap of dead leaves which hides it.

[235] We are astonished when we find someone who claims to believe that an evil spirit dwells in a certain oak tree, or that there is a God who hears our prayers and loves us. What can they mean? What are they up to, saying that these things are the case, when plainly, in

all the ways they otherwise accept for things being or not being the case, these things are *not* the case?

Imagine someone from a tribe which had no notion of pictorial representation. Mighn't he be astonished when he came up against our belief that certain coloured smears on canvas 'showed' living people? He gazes at us in amazement as we are moved by one portrait, and amused by another. Don't we realize that human beings are complex structures of protein, and that most of the colours we are looking at on the canvas are not even organic?

The portraits are interesting to us precisely because they are done in paint instead of flesh. It's the same with the myths. Their discontinuity with experienced life, with normal logic – the fact that they are plainly done in another material – is what gives them their otherness.

36] Although explanations within the scientific canon are scientific, there is undoubtedly a mythology of science – a belief that science offers a general explanation, brings all the parts of the universe into relationship. Everything, we feel, is in theory predictable, and can be accounted for by definite laws. What makes this belief so believable is our patent inability to predict even our own behaviour, and our experience of life not as the neutral operation of objective laws, but as a subjective process of observation, feeling, decision and action.

[237]   Mathematical myths, logical myths. Behind the
confusion of material things, existing before the
universe began and surviving after it ends, are
certain hypothetical truths . . .

[238]   'It's as if there were a father, who loved and punished
us, and to whom we could turn . . .' And the chaos
seems reassuring, like a family home. However
terrible the punishments and disasters, we feel that
they are not unlimited, not out of all control, but part
of a pattern of life whose ultimate aim is to cherish us.
    'It's as if there were an inevitable historical process .
And now the chaos seems like a gigantic machine. The
apparently unconnected movements of the parts have
an air of purposiveness, just as they do when we look
into a complicated machine which we don't
understand. We can't see how the up-and-down
movements of this valve fit in with the eccentric
cyclical jerks of that wheel. We only know that,
because it's a machine, they must.

[239]   I see a face in the piled clouds. It soars up
triumphantly from the complex mass, as if leading it,
touched with a strange golden serenity by the rays of
the setting sun. Now everything begins to fall into
place around it. A golden army is following it out of
the west; the broken remnants of a dark enemy are
fleeing before them to the north . . .

o] You smile at my hackneyed romanticism. When *you* look (you tell me) you see nothing but plain heaps of water vapour. I take my revenge by smiling at your hackneyed scientism. I am metaphoring the scene emotionally up, into a range of associations with feeling. You are metaphoring the scene emotionally down, into an undisturbing world of kettles and engines and simple science books you read as a child.

1] We need only a hint – one eye, and the line of the cheek, or a vague recollection of the dry tone of an old textbook – and we are away, filling in the whole picture with lightning strokes.

2] We believe in our myths. Yet we know, in that secret part of the mind which knows what we ourselves cannot allow ourselves to know, that they are fictions. This is why we are reduced to believing in them.

3] You're like a government. You have to maintain some consistent identity, some coherent behaviour, in your relationships with the many people around you. You need to maintain some stable shape and attitude in a shifting world. You must evolve slowly. Speaking privately together, Ministers are as responsive, sceptical and dubious as anyone else. Speaking corporately, as a government, they cannot recognize these inconsistencies – cannot even feel them.

[244]   The trouble starts when you are forced to take account
        of this discrepancy.
            It's as if you were sitting in a room absent-mindedly
        picking your nose and making symphonic noises
        through your teeth. You're aware that you're doing it,
        and that you wouldn't be doing it if there were anyone
        around to see, but not too aware, because your mind is
        on other things. Then suddenly you realize that there
        is a mirror in which you can see your reflection. At
        once you're forced to pay full attention to what you're
        doing. You have to stop, or continue in full
        awareness of a double standard for public and private
        behaviour, or perhaps even resolve to make picking
        your nose and shushing Brahms's Fourth Symphony
        through you teeth a consistent part of your whole life,
        public as well as private.

[245]   When someone is converted from his myth, the
        occasion may be external, but the force it releases is
        internal. He feels that really he has known all along.
            The vehemence of the convert is striking. He is mak
        up for having hitherto deceived *himself*.

[246]   Sometimes myths die slowly around us, like
        dilapidated old houses which we go on living in even
        as the tiles fall off the roof and the stairs give way.
        Sometimes we're out of one myth and into another
        without even realizing it: on the 22nd we are arguing
        that the society we live in is based upon the concept of

individual liberty; at a dinner party on the 25th we hear ourselves insisting that the behaviour of the individual is socially determined. But we've always got some myth to live in – we don't stay out at night, under the great emptiness of the sky. And at first our new myth (just like a new house!) looks ideal. We've always wanted smaller rooms, we discover. We've always wanted to live further away from the shops, with mock half-timbering and pebble-dash!

7] A sensation of spiritual movement (whether progress or decline) is maintained among the community at large by its journeying on from myth to myth, from metaphor to metaphor.

We have moved, in particular, from one aspect of human relationships to another in our search for a metaphor of the whole. At different times we have caught glimpses of some essential principle in the fear inspired by an overbearing father, the love we might feel for a benevolent one, the bonds of obligation and affection between brothers, the sense of ecstasy or epiphany, the sense of guilt, the possibilities of supremacy and submission. The material of these metaphors was part of our experience from the beginning of time, but the burden of general significance has been shifted restlessly from one to another, as a man shifts an awkward load from right shoulder to left shoulder, from shoulders to back.

[248] The people who move us from myth to myth are like
       the reformers who hoped to cure all social ills by
       taking people out of the slums, which were the context
       of their diseases and crimes, and installing them in
       new, disease- and crime-free housing estates. It was a
       terrible blow to discover that these estates in their
       turn developed a characteristic pattern of social
       disorder.

[249] You can translate out of the German, or out of the
       Aramaic. But only into another language! Not into
       the world of which the language treats!
          Moving from one myth to another is in some ways a
       little like translating between languages. A particular
       language has its own idioms, its own voice; a
       topography which favours certain ways of speaking,
       and makes others awkward.

[250] Like the proverbial bad workman we blame our tools –
       money, arithmetic, science, technology, mythology.
       They're enslaving us, we cry. And our tools *do*
       dictate the form of our life. Think of a pneumatic
       drill. Of lace-making needles. Of a microphone. Of a
       ship. Of our ten fingers.

[251] Of course, the word 'myth' is belittling. The point
       about (say) Christian myths to the Christian is that
       they're *not* myths. When I say that I find Christian
       myths deep and compelling, this isn't the same thing
       at all. In my interest in them as myths I step back out

of this mythology and into another – the mythology of myths, perhaps. (A common modern mythology.)

2] I tell you that our religions and philosophies are metaphors. The tone of my voice suggests that I in my turn am kindly ushering you towards a hygienic new tower-block. But my pronouncement is itself a metaphor. It pictures these difficult abstractions in another material. It gives a feeling of concreteness, offers the possibility of coming at them, by assimilating them into the range of familiar literary techniques.

I might go on to say this: 'My saying, "Our religions and philosophies are metaphors is itself a metaphor," is a metaphor in its turn . . .'

The metaphorability of the universe is bottomless. *Everything* can be pressed into service in its turn to stand for something else.

3] Holy texts are holy because they are rich metaphors, into which much can be read. But the converse is also true: they are rich metaphors because they are holy. Their holiness focuses our imagination upon them, and produces in us the expectation and intention of finding them thick with metaphor. Any text (even Patience Strong), any object (even a chair), can seem to glow with a deep inner light if it is pronounced holy and subjected to this sort of attention. The mistranslations in holy texts reverberate as suggestively as the rest.

[254]   The trouble with modern theologians is that they've caught sight of themselves in the mirror. They elected to go on shushing through their teeth, and to justify it publicly by claiming that it's a thoroughly scientific exercise in voice-production and harmony. The embarrassing statements about God which they utter are really, they now claim, statements about Ultimate Reality and the Ground of our Being, which makes them sound at any rate entirely unanthropomorphic. But radiating still from this neutral stuff, they feel obliged to insist, is some kind of unagented but personal love.

    Mythology is sustained metaphor; and the most terrible nonsense occurs when metaphors get mixed. 'He lost his head and closed his eyes to the consequences.' 'Ultimate Reality sent its only begotten son.'

[255]   I should like to say this: don't *worry* when you find yourself in the midst of a mythology. Relax and enjoy it! Sit in one mythology, and put your feet up on another! You'll still be tied up in *some* myth even if you get out of this one. And after all, you know how to enjoy fairy stories without translating wands into phalluses all the time, and handsome princes into members of the feudal oppressor class. (At least, I hope you do.) You can read a novel without wondering anxiously all the time whether it's true or false. You understand in what way it's true that Kuznetzov was

at Borodino, and in what way it's true that Pierre was.

Live mythologies up to the hilt, like the old woman Sinyavsky writes about, who cries to her son when he tries to cut her toenails for her, 'How can you think of such a thing, Kostik! How can you? It's time for me to die. And how am I going to climb the mountain up to God without my toenails?'

[6] We think of memories as being like inward photographs or movies. But as soon as you bring any of these pictures before your mind you notice this overwhelming difference: the detail in them is not specific.

I bring a particular event to mind. It's something that I remember very clearly, one of those scenes which are said to be 'etched upon the memory', a frightening moment when I thought I might be killed. I was aboard an aircraft landing in the dark one winter evening. Three tyres burst on touchdown, and looking back out of a window at the front of the passenger cabin I saw first a great shower of sparks pouring back in our slipstream, then a brilliant sheet of flame. It was coming up from the wheels, but in the darkness it looked as if it were an engine on fire.

When I first glimpse it in my mind, the whole scene seems vivid and definite. I can recall looking round at my fellow-passengers to see if they had noticed; then looking further back to spot the nearest emergency exit. I can recall a feeling of inevitability. But the more

I examine the scene, the more it slips away beyond the corner of my eye. For instance, I recall *that* I was sitting at the front of the plane. But was it at the very front? As I turn my head once again in memory, from the sheet of flame outside the window to my neighbours inside, it does not traverse a bulkhead, or another row of seats. I recall *that* my neighbours showed no sign of having noticed anything wrong; but there are no particular faces in my head to establish this. I recall *that* I felt, 'Well, if you travel regularly by air, you're bound to get killed sooner or later;' but as soon as I set the words down I begin to suspect that they didn't go through my head at the time, and that they are the verbalization that I used later, when I told the story, to indicate how I had felt.

Now, even as I notice these lacunae, I rush to fill the I see a bulkhead as I turned, finished in a grained cream plastic material. I see the profile of the man sitting next to me – dark hair, distinct beard-shadow. I experiment with feeling various kinds of heaviness and resignation. But equally, I realize, without any damage to the structure of the scene I can turn and see a row of seats, two rows of seats, four rows; and a smooth pink profile as hairless as a baby's. I can feel my feeling of inevitability as a kind of lightness.

What I shall never forget, though, is the appearance the sheet of flame itself. Nothing but darkness, and a bright orange mass trailing back in the wind of the plane's passage . . . But even as I picture it I realize that this *can't* have been exactly what I saw. The landing lights must have been on! From where I was sitting there must have been a brilliant spotlight visible in the leading edge of the wing, somewhere above the flames, casting a white beam forwards into the darkness. Now that I have realized this intellectually, I fill the detail in at once; now I see the scene with the white light as well as the orange flame. But that's not how I saw it when it came to mind in all its initial clarity and vividness.

7] I know what this reminds me of – writing. When I write a scene in a novel I embody the skeleton of the event in the flesh of particularity which suggests itself. Davis is to go from the Foreign Office to the German Embassy. He could go by taxi; be driven by his colleague Askenaugh; or just arrive. But I find it best to discover that 'He walked across the park in the winter sunshine, obscurely irritated by the chattering of the birds in the bare trees.' And there he is in my mind, vivid and definite, with the cold light slightly dazzling him, and the birdsong sounding out-of-place and meaningless in his ears. But when I revise the chapter this doesn't quite catch the tone I want. I decide that 'He walked across the park through a grey fog that was entangled in the trees like a sodden paper bag. Even the birds had been reduced to silence.' And now that I've decided this, it is so.

8] Someone asks me what colour eyes a character in one of my novels has; I never mentioned it in the book.

A moment's thought, and I supply an answer. What did my moment's thought consist of? Remembering, inventing, deciding, or deducing? Not exactly any of these; not exactly all combined.

[259] Now I'm trying to remember some one particular concrete thing that I've forgotten. (Someone's name, let's say.) It's on the tip of my tongue. I almost have it! It's . . . But just as I'm about to grasp it, it recedes into the shadows again, like the ghost of Hamlet's father.

But this is *weird*! Something without shape or conte is seeking flesh, like a spirit seeking a body to inhabit. A nothingness, a void, indescribable – yet I'll know at once when the word to fit it turns up. I know it's not Williams or Bolton or Plater. It's something a bit like Klimt . . . Irvingrude somehow comes near it, or Ermyntrude . . . I have a feeling somehow of women crossing a lawn, in long skirts, in sunlight . . . of complicated love-letters from Rainer-Maria Rilke . . .

Hildegard! Of course! Hildegard, Hildegard, Hildegard! How could I forget such an odd surname?

I try to imagine what sort of computer it would be th remembered things in this kind of way, and nothing comes to mind at all. It's not like searching through files, or matching (say) photographs with descriptions. It's more like the feeling you get sometimes of having a great thought, or a great book, on the tip of your tongue. You feel the charm, the sense of excitement, before any particular outline presents itself. (When it does, the charm fades.)

Now that I've said that, I've begun to doubt if Hildegard is the word I meant at all. Hildegard . . . No, it doesn't *begin* to be it! It doesn't come near it!

[60] Memories are like legends, private legends. They take particular form when they are told – and when they are told again they are made incarnate in a different body. Now the hero has an iron helmet, now a golden one. In this version he spends a night in a Chapel Perilous, in that it's a year in the wilderness. In some versions he is Gawain, in others Parsifal.

One might put it like this: legends are not about particular people or particular places. They are about certain aspects of human nature and human destiny, and they are expressed *in terms of* particular people and particular places. So with memories. They are not about the house where I was born, or the state of the starboard landing-gear on a particular B.E.A. Vanguard one particular winter evening. They are about fear, and desolation, and resignation to fate, and pleasure, and disgust, and arousal, and security – all the different twinges and spasms and colourations which are at the heart of our experience, and which we struggle to make concrete, and accessible to consideration. They are expressed *in terms of* the events through which we have lived.

[261]   The point is not that the necessity makes the plot possible, but that the plot makes manifest the sense of necessity.

   A great wind blows over the land. It's through the resistance of the trees and the dance of the fallen leaves that we see it.

[262]   If we had no experience of a world external to us, we should have no experience of ourselves, either. Our relationship with the world is that intimate!

[263]   It astonishes me that it has ever been possible in practice to undertake the analysis of dreams in terms of Freudian symbolism. My dreams are never specific enough to make this kind of literal one-to-one translation (purse = vagina; stairs = intercourse, etc.) even begin to seem plausible. A dream disappears as you tell it; the more exact you try to be, the more you realize it's eluded you. 'I came to this lighted house, and there was this staircase going up . . .' But even as you say it, you realize that 'lighted house' and 'staircase' scarcely begin to come at it, since it was not only dark but also broad daylight, not only a house but also a gigantic air-liner; and that the experience of going up the stairs was also simultaneously, or alternatively, the experience of walking across a wide, flat beach crossed by sand-yachts, or perhaps flown over by men in early biplanes. The selection of words to come at this shifting, ambiguous manifold is almost

arbitrary. In effect you're making your account up, as I did with my account of Mr Davis's walk from the Foreign Office to the German Embassy – and making it up *wrong*. Even the identity of the individuals one meets in dreams wanders and doubles up on itself. The words they speak to us, which affect us with such remorse and joy and longing, have every meaning and none – no form that can be written down in the morning.

54] The dream disappears not only as we put it into words, but even as we attempt to recall it inside our own heads. I wake in the morning, and a sense that something has happened weighs on me. I lie there, looking at the daylight round the edge of the curtains, and try to put images to this feeling of having dreamed. Even as I do so, I know they're not right. They're too specific. They don't catch the unremarked ambiguity of the dream. Already they're back-constructions, a plausible fleshing-out of the dream feeling. And this is happening where the operation is entirely internal! Where the material and the notation are both apparently the same kind of stuff (my own mental images), and where there could really be a one-to-one correlation, if ever such a correlation were possible.

65] How else can I express my experience to myself, if not in words, if not in memories? But the fiction that I'm creating doesn't look accurate or adequate even to *me*.

[266]   I dreamt that my wife was driving a bus in Moscow.
Did I recognize it as Moscow from its appearance? No
it looked rather like London, if anything. Did I deduce
from some other evidence that it must be Moscow,
something somebody said, perhaps? No, I just *knew* it
was Moscow. She was driving the bus by operating
two levers, like the controls of a crane. Did I see the
two levers? I don't think I did. I just knew there were
two levers. Did I see my wife? I think I recall seeing
her face. But I also think that I knew it was my wife
before I saw her face. I think I saw her face *because* I
knew it was her.

   In what sense did I *know* all these things? Was it a p
of my dream that the actual words of propositions
went through my head – 'This is Moscow', 'The bus is
being driven by my wife', 'She is driving it with two
levers'? I don't think any words went through my head
at all. Did I know them in the way I know that
$7 \times 7 = 49$, or that Reykjavik is the capital of Iceland?
Not really. I know that I know *these* things because
I've used the knowledge on occasions. I didn't have to
produce the knowledge that it was Moscow my wife
was driving the bus in until now, and I knew that I
knew it already, in the dream. I was *aware* of its being
Moscow. It was somehow at the back of my mind. Or
perhaps not so much at the back of my mind as at the
back of the picture.

[267]   Of course, when I was actually in Moscow I knew I
was in Moscow. No propositions went through my

head to this effect, but I was aware that I was in Moscow, and this awareness affected my whole experience of the city. But my awareness in this case *arose* from that experience. I was very conscious of being in Moscow because I'd planned to go there, and bought tickets, and got up early to get on a plane . . . In the dream there was no evidence for this haunting general sense; but the sense was so strong that it informed and permeated even experience which contradicted it.

8] Gold-edged clouds pile up on a summer's evening. You have a sense of grandeur; of the heart opening; of other days in other years. Do you *see* this? No. Deduce it? Certainly not.

9] You notice a man on the other side of the restaurant. He's neat-featured and self-contained. He carries conviction. For a moment you feel, if only *you* could be like that . . .

Then suddenly you realize, with a weird sense of shock, that it's an old friend.

Now he looks entirely different!

70] A familiar dream situation: I dream of a fire breaking out, and of a firebell insistently ringing, and then wake to find that the alarm-clock is going off. I have the feeling that reality has broken into my dreaming, and that I have interpreted that reality in the context of the dream. I see a clear distinction between the factitiousness of the dream and the givenness of the ringing. I'd like to shrug my shoulders and say that I really heard a real ringing, that the only thing I added was an explanation.

But the firebell in my dream was a great brass thing, rung by a rope from its clapper! It didn't sound at all like an alarm-clock!

I feel on examination that I've drawn the line of demarcation between the given and the factitious at the wrong point. A noise was supplied from the outside, certainly, and an explanation from the inside. But the explanation (as it were) reached out to the noise; the actual hearing was itself interpretative.

I dreamed one night, when our children were young, that the second child was crying – a characteristic and unmistakable soprano *sostenuto*. I woke and found that there was indeed a child crying, but that it was the third, a baby still, with a no less characteristic pattern of short phrases wept contralto. What I'd taken in from outside was not (so to speak) 'the actual sound', but the *idea* of a child crying, the general sense, the international crying-child symbol; and I'd then heard this by constructing my own picture of a particular child making a particular crying.

[271] There is a similar carry-over of sense rather than form in the case recorded by Freud of the woman who dreamt repeatedly that marriage was a game. She knew Greek, as Freud deduced, and the Greek for marriage is *gamos*.

I once dreamt that I was at a dinner party in Arnold Wesker's house. In so far as anything is anything in a dream, the house was round. The association is plain enough *now* (Wesker's connection with the Round House Theatre); but during the course of the dream the roundness went without either explanation or conjecture.

72] The narrative which comes closest to capturing the feel of a dream is not about a dream at all. It's Stendhal's account of how Fabrice del Dongo galloped with Marshal Ney's party through the battle of Waterloo. Just as you would in a dream, Fabrice arrives ludicrously unprepared, without the slightest idea of what a soldier in battle is expected to do, relying on seeing what the men around him do and doing the same. He has a dream-like sense of being in a false position, trying to say nothing that he has not worked out carefully in advance for fear that his Italian accent and syntax will get him arrested as a spy. When he arrives, the battle is already taking place. He picks his way through the countryside towards the sound of cannon – towards the battle of Waterloo as an already established historical fact. The first thing that happens to him is that he falls in with the escort of a party of generals, led by Ney. He doesn't know which one is Ney; he just knows that one is. They gallop furiously through the complexities of the battlefield. Fabrice doesn't know where they are galloping. There is just galloping, and events about them. Now there

are sprays of earth coming up nearby – bullets,
Fabrice works out. Now there are redcoats dead on the
ground. Now they are reining in because Napoleon is
going by – Fabrice can't actually see him, he just hears
the hussars around him shout '*Vive l'Empereur!*' Now
they are in the mud of the covered way; now in a dyke
full of water. Now Fabrice is drunk on *eau-de-vie*.
Now the hussars around him are getting killed. Now
they are taking his horse. Now he is back with the
vivandière he left when he first arrived. A great deal of
time has elapsed. But what informs and charges the
whole sequence of disconnected events is the
dreamlike sense that *this is the battle of Waterloo*. One
sees mud, mud, bullets, drunkenly; one knows
Waterloo.

[273]   To philosophers, delusion has been merely the chaff
from which the grain of real perception had to be
winnowed. But delusion is a *case* of perception, and a
suggestive one. When you actually sit with a sick man
who complains about the presence of lions in the room
traditional philosophical talk about hallucination seems
beside the point. 'Experiencing sense-data which are
unrelated to the sense-data experienced by other
observers . . .' 'Falsely inferring from his perceptions
that . . .' It's much more as if he just *knows* there are
lions in the room, as you yourself might declare that
the room was filled with melancholy, or was too small.
Perhaps he goes on looking at the flowers, and doesn't

see anything lion-like at all; or perhaps this general assumption of lions charges everything he sees with the presence of lions. Perhaps you, oppressed by the melancholy of the room, look at the thermometer in an entirely practical way, and see just the relationship of the mercury and the gradations; or perhaps you see hopelessness in the pattern of the wallpaper, the scattered small possessions on the chest of drawers.

4] A note sounds, and the grains of sand on the tray jump into a certain characteristic pattern of standing waves. Now another note sounds, and the sand forms a new picture.

5] Two small insanities of my own. The first was when I was still at school, and playing a great deal of chess. I began to see people in the street as being in chess relationships to each other. That man standing second in the bus queue and that bus-inspector standing level with the stop on the opposite side of the pavement, I would realize with anxiety, were a knight's move away from each other; if the man didn't move he would be taken. Then I would notice, with relief, that he was in fact covered by the woman in the shop doorway, on the diagonal from him. Did the bus-inspector look like a knight? No; – I just knew he was, from the fact that he was standing a knight's move away from his victim. Did I see the pavement laid out in squares? Is this how I knew it was a knight's move? No – I knew it was a knight's move because it was a knight threatening the man.

The second craziness came upon me quite recently. began to see almost everyone around me (including myself, in the mirror) as looking like a boy I was once at school with. He was someone who was an amusing companion, but never a close friend. After I left that particular school, at the age of twelve, I never thought about him again, until our paths crossed briefly six years ago. And suddenly, here was everyone looking like him! The same suggestion of a tip-tilted nose, with a high forehead above it . . . It was as clear as if we'd all had labels on us with his name on them.

Am I trying to tell you that the people around me ceased to look like themselves? Not at all. They looked just as much like themselves as they always had! This was what was so disturbing. But they *also* looked like old Good. All those various noses, hooked, bulbous, flattened, suddenly looked tip-tilted? All those foreheads, low, receding, covered by fringes, suddenly looked high? I could see the tip-tiltedness and highnes concealed in them all, because I could see that the faces looked like Good's.

[276] A small child talking. A long speech, with only occasional words and phrases that overlap with any known language, or perhaps none. And yet, from the child's solemnity or laughter, from its gestures, from the actions it performs as it speaks, one cannot but feel

that there is a general sense behind its words. It's not
that there are definite thoughts which it cannot
translate into language; without the words there can
be no word-thoughts. One might put it like this: I
read into the gabble of sound a general tone or
relationship (to a doll, for instance). So does the child;
reads it, or writes it there, or both.

7] For hundreds of pages the closely-reasoned arguments
unroll, axioms and theorems interlock. And what
remains with us at the end? A general sense that the
world can be expressed in closely-reasoned arguments,
in interlocking axioms and theorems. (As it might be,
with another sort of book, a general sense of
inscrutable fate or of human responsibility, or of the
presence of lions.)

8] The other day I read an article in the paper by a man I
know listing all the reasons which had made him give
up wearing contact lenses and go back to spectacles.
I remember talking to him when he was still wearing
the contact lenses, and his telling me the same list of
drawbacks and disasters as a kind of humorous aside,
while strongly advising me to get rid of my own
spectacles and be fitted with contact lenses, too. On
both occasions, I've no doubt, he was entirely sincere.
This is the way one makes one's mind up, and changes
it. It's like a water mobile I once saw, with eccentric
scoops which filled with water until quite suddenly

they tipped up and emptied. It was one last small drop
that overbalanced each scoop; but in the moment of
overbalancing the whole body of accumulated water
shifted and flung its weight behind the movement as
well, as if some violent internal force had been
released.

[279] Yesterday I disliked him, because of his frivolousness
and inconstancy, his voice, and his extraordinary,
maddening laugh.
    Today I like him, because of his gaiety and
unpredictability, his voice, and his extraordinary
laugh that some people find so maddening.

[280] Why worry about the indefiniteness of memory and
dreams? The kind of experience which has interested
philosophers is our perception of what at this moment
lies before our eyes. The distinction seems quite clear
until I turn from thinking about what lies before my
eyes to actually looking at it. At once I am brought up
against one simple physical characteristic of the eye:
the extreme narrowness of the angle of intense vision
(about one degree). Even to take in the back of my
hand, twelve inches in front of my face, my eye has to
dart to and fro; so that in my present experience of
this one limited object I'm at any one moment
remembering several hundred times as much as I'm
actually seeing. (Work out the mathematics of it
yourself!) And already, looking at this one quite small,

very familiar object, our experience has the same
structure as the memory and the dream – the sense of a
whole, but a curious lack of specific content. You
raise your eyebrows at this last suggestion. Look at the
back of your hand. Now, how many tendons are
visible? How many veins? At once, as soon as I ask the
questions, you see the answers (rather as I rushed to
fill in details of the aircraft in my memory, as soon as I
realized they were missing). But you *hadn't* seen them
before I asked; these fundamental aspects of the scene
had not become part of your experience of it. And now
I ask: how many hairs are there? How many
granulations of the skin? And these aspects you *still*
can't see, even though I've drawn your attention to
them, even though you're looking, even though you
can see every single hair and every single granulation.

Perhaps you'll reply that putting a number to a
collection is a technical development over and above
purely being aware of the collection. Let's take another
aspect, then. Can you see the colour of your hand?
Yes, in general. But we're not concerned with the
general – we're trying to be specific. And now you
look specifically you see that it's extraordinarily
complicated; pink tones spreading back from the
knuckles, white where the light catches the high point
of each granulation . . . Before I drew your attention
to it you hadn't *begun* to see this – and you can't take it
all in even now.

And how many tendons are visible? You have to make

a quick check again! It's staring you in the eye, your attention has already been drawn to it – and it had disappeared like yesterday!

[281] When you try to think about perception, your attention is distracted by knowing a little about optics. Simple diagrams come into your mind showing the similarity of the eye and the camera, with rays of light from a little man passing through the lens to form an image of him, miniaturized but complete, on the retina or the ground-glass screen.

This is why phenomenalists thought they might be able to purge perceptual language of its interpretative implications, and get down to the real stuff of the world, by analysing statements about pennies (it was always pennies!) into statements about elliptical brown sense-data. It's difficult to believe that anyone ever thought 'brown ellipse' might be less interpretative than 'penny'. They were distracted by knowing that, when they looked at a penny, there must be inside their eye this tiny brown elliptical patch of light. And because it was clearly this tiny brown elliptical patch of light which was transformed into the electrical messages to the brain, they began to think of perception as the brain looking at the retina (or the mind looking at the contents of the brain).

The tiny brown elliptical patch of light on the retina would of course be upside down. Curiously, phenomenalists always seemed to have their sense-data the right way up.

] When I say that the content of your perception is not as specific as you like to imagine, I don't mean that it's not sharp, like a blurred photograph, or that it's unresolved, in the way that detail might be beyond the resolution of a lens. Your view of the back of your hand is technically superb. A phenomenalist might just as well get himself entangled in quantum mechanics as in optics. He might just as well begin to worry that the real basic material was not the flat patches of light on the retina, but the electromagnetic quanta by which they are transmitted to the brain. This would produce an elegant new language. We could replace 'I am experiencing an elliptical brown sense-datum' with 'I am undergoing an elliptical brown burst of electrical activity'.

You can look at the back of your hand (hand-coloured patches of light on retina, hand-coloured differences of electrical potential along the optic nerve) and, if your thoughts are elsewhere, see *nothing*.

3] What makes the idea of 'sense-data' philosophically attractive is the feeling that the fundamental question is: 'What exists?' (The ontological view of the universe.) How has this weird question grown in our minds to such general importance? We don't ask very often from a practical point of view whether something exists or not. How many times in the past year have you needed to know the answer to such a question? And what a static universe the question suggests! It doesn't seem much like the one we struggle with each day, where we try to understand what's going on, then try to stop it or help it continue, where we see a continuous process of change, and where we continuously change our conception of even the most static and enduring features. Even the more sophisticated question, 'What is the case?' to which it was at one time thought that sense-data statements might provide plausible answers, has an artificial air when we make its application universal. This conception of things was destroyed by Heisenberg, for a start, when he demonstrated (in the Indeterminacy Principle) that for an object in motion no theoretically complete account of what was the case (no statement with equal exactitude of both its position and its velocity) could ever be given.

[284] Talking about 'sense-data' suggests an idea of perception (that our perceptions of external objects are somehow constructed out of perceptual atoms) which is largely back to front. You read a passage in a book and at the end of it you have a picture in your mind, or an argument, or a certain feeling. Is that picture (or that argument, or that feeling) a construction from the meanings of the individual words in the passage? Not at all – the meanings of the individual words depended largely on the context. The whole gives meaning to the parts. You read in phrases, in sentences, in paragraphs. When you read something in a language you don't know well, piecing it together word by word

you have to go back at the end of each section– in your mind at any rate – and read it as a whole.

Fire a flashgun in a darkened room – an electronic flash, say, illuminating the room for only a ten-thousandth of a second. Do you see some kind of uninterpreted perceptual elements? Not at all. Already you see a *something*.

5] Words evoke. They call out something *within ourselves*.

So does what lies before our eyes. To put it wrongly, but not entirely wrongly, we see leaf, leaf, root, branch, and in the same instant dream a forest.

The surgeon touches two electrodes to the patient's brain. Now *he* sees a forest, as well.

6] Seeing, when you think about it, is in a curious way like saying. When you look at your hand, you can tell me anything about it that I wish to know, or anything that you wish me to know, or anything that strikes you about it. In the same way, you can see anything that I direct your attention to, or anything that you direct your attention to, or anything that catches your attention. There is no totality, or generality, of things you can say or see about your hand. Both your saying and your seeing are selective and interpretative.

7] To see something is to make oneself a private metaphor of it. (I'm speaking metaphorically!) The metaphor might be a visual one: I see the shifting vapour as a face, I see my hand as a hand. Or it might be a propositional one: I look at the back of my hand and see *that* when I raise my thumb the tendon appears in just this particular way.

(*What* particular way? – *This* particular way. – What kind of a proposition is this supposed to be, where you end up by pointing? You might as well ask what kind of proposition is 'Socrates is a man', which starts off by pointing.)

[288] You want to object that *of course* you see your hand as a hand. No 'of course' about it. You lay in your cot when you were a little younger, and your eyes fastened on this pink object floating in front of them, and you frowned with the effort of making some sense of it.

The likeness of your hand to a hand has got trodden down into the subsoil of your perception just as the metaphors for mental states have got trodden down into your thinking about yourself.

[289] In perception, at any rate, God proposes and Man disposes.

[290] Modern visionaries wish to liberate us from our 'Western' preoccupation with ordering and dominating the world around us. They want us to be able to live humbly with the rest of creation, accepting it, in harmony with it, in comradeship with it. This is a townsman's view of nature, which fails to notice that nature is in fact engaged in a never-ending labour of

self-definition and self-ordering through the struggle to survive. It's also a mechanistic view of human perception, as a passive receptacle for the world like the light-sensitive surface in a camera.

In a recent film about this kind of 'liberation', the hero, as he symbolically breaks down walls and makes love to his sister, also abandons language, and expresses himself instead in grunts and squeaks. And it's true; if it were imaginable that we could achieve this kind of 'liberation', language would certainly have to go, because language in its very essence is an instrument for ordering, codifying and controlling. And in the end perception would have to go, too. In seeing (with fitting ecstasy) the green leaves of the tree against the blueness of the sky we are already interpreting, selecting, slicing, cutting, ignoring, arranging, rendering down.

91] A novel which gives a minute and circumstantial account of Parisian society in the 1840s, or a crowded painting of the Last Judgment with every detail realized, and into them I read a general sense of corrupt social energy, of apocalypse. Two lines of a poem, as precisely placed as the surgeon's electrodes ('And characters in long coats/Deep in the litter baskets'), and into them I read a world of detail and circumstance.

92] A strange sight in the street, something we can't quite understand, and we come running.

A woman with enamelled skin, blank eyes lost in kohl who smiles slightly and says nothing; and for a time, at any rate, men see in her everything they hope to see in women. And here's a woman with an odd sort of look, who has a way of saying weird random things that fall into her head – there's something that men see in her, too.

The most beautiful women of all are the ones going away from us in the street, whose faces we never see at all.

[293] No building is ever quite as beautiful as it was when it stood unfinished and half-hidden in scaffolding; not, at any rate, until it lies in ruins, and its last weathered stones are set in lawns laid and maintained by the Department of the Environment.

No author's works are as deep and comprehensive as those of the ancient Greek whose extant writings consist of five words, 'A dry soul is best.'

[294] The future is the cloud of all clouds, into which *anything* can be read. It comprises all the complexity of the present – every tree, every breath, every instant of the history of every cubic centimetre of the universe up to now – rearranged by ourselves, and by forces which are not ourselves, into any pattern our hopes or fears suggest.

We see apocalypses in it, and visions of the present extended without alteration, and cities of gold in which everything is better than everything else and everyone is unremittingly joyful (all the laws of logic repealed at last). The only thing we never quite manage to see is the present which the future does in time become; a present so oddly probable and predictable, so strangely improbable and unpredicted.

95] The past seems so deep to us because we read into it (often ironically) the present which developed out of it. Its possibilities are clear, as the possibilities of the present are still obscure. In an odd way, the present as we read it into the past may be more real to us than the present as we actually experience it.

96] Nor does our nostalgia need definite content. We can feel the most intense yearning for scenes we cannot quite recall, for feelings we cannot quite recollect, for experiences we cannot quite specify. Our nostalgia is often strongest and sweetest for things which never were part of our life at all. No one aches so much for the lost glories of the pre-1914 world as those who were just too young to remember it; or for the lost sweetness of summer weekends at the great country houses as those too poor ever to have been invited.

97] You can even feel nostalgia for the present. Think of those serene, sunlit days in late September, when you seem to be living already with the memory of summer. Characters in books sometimes say what in life we half feel: – 'I shall always remember this moment.' By a literary device they are remembering it already – enjoying it by standing back from it and yearning after it with outstretched arms.

[298] You're a cloud, and you rely on me to see a face in you.

[299] When you're attracted to someone (sexually, socially – it's the same kind of thing) that person becomes translucent, edged with light, as a cloud does when it moves into the track of the sun. For a time, at any rate, all those vaporous whorls and ambiguities become as definite and brilliant as burnished metal.
     'What can he see in her?' What can he see in the clouds? Some heartbreaking suggestion of a golden day in the reign of William IV, fleeting away downwind.

[300] Our friends absorb us because of their complexity – their depths, their ambiguity, the endlessly changing sum of their actions and attitudes. We read them over and over again, now this way, now that; as (among other things) metaphors of ourselves.

[301] What makes the world of interest to us, what involves us with it, what constitutes our pleasure in it, is its metaphoricality.
     Comfort is a metaphor. And the performing of tasks. And producing an effect upon things. And having an effect produced by things upon oneself.

02] The legibility of things constitutes their savour.

03] I don't mean that things are a clue to a savour, or that they represent a pleasure. The savour is in the act of reading them.

04] The religious believe that the world is of interest because it is a manifestation of God, because God can be perceived in it. Or this is what they believe that they believe. But it is the act of perception that really engages them; not God, but the seeing of the world *as* God. At the very moment when they expect to see God face to face, without the mediation of the physical world, without this act of reading, life ceases.

05] Nothing in the explicit arts speaks to us with the same intimacy as music. From a hundred and a hundred and fifty years ago it comes to us like a familiar voice in the next room, or like a voice in a dream which you understand completely without there being any actual words. You know that if you could turn your head and see who it was, he would be wearing the most extraordinary archaic clothes; that if you could make out the words you'd realize his head was full of the most extraordinary archaic notions. And yet, as you listen, tears of pure happiness come to your eyes.

06] And more poignant still is music half-heard and half-remembered.

[307]   If the physical world ceased to exist, painting and poetry and prose would become meaningless. But you can't help feeling wistfully, as you do about logic and mathematics, that the possibilities of harmony and counterpoint would linger on in the silence.

[308]   And the glory of writing is its dependence upon the world – the necessity it puts us in of coming back again and again to confront the complexity of what lies before our eyes.

[309]   The clouds clear, and there beyond them, stretching to the outermost limits of the fleeing universe, are more clouds: galaxies, mists made up of droplets of matter condensed out from the hot primeval gases. Perhaps each galaxy is a puff of steam left behind by cosmic locomotives racing away from us faster than light. Perhaps, on one of those cold, bright mornings when your breath condenses, God wandered through the universe, saying a word here and a word there. What he said was what people say to us in dreams.
   Or perhaps he was humming to himself. A phrase here – and that was Andromeda. Then he pottered on a couple of million light-years, abstracted, and hummed us, and all the Milky Way around us.